Happiness in Life and After Death:

An Islamic Sufi View

First published by O Books, 2010
O Books is an imprint of John Hunt Publishing Ltd., The Bothy, Deershot Lodge, Park Lane, Ropley,
Hants, SO24 0BE, UK
office1@o-books.net
www.o-books.net

Distribution in:

UK and Europe
Orca Book Services
orders@orcabookservices.co.uk
Tel: 01202 665432 Fax: 01202 666219
Int. code (44)

USA and Canada
NBN
custserv@nbnbooks.com
Tel: 1 800 462 6420 Fax: 1 800 338 4550

Australia and New Zealand
Brumby Books
sales@brumbybooks.com.au
Tel: 61 3 9761 5535 Fax: 61 3 9761 7095

Far East (offices in Singapore, Thailand,
Hong Kong, Taiwan)
Pansing Distribution Pte Ltd
kemal@pansing.com
Tel: 65 6319 9939 Fax: 65 6462 5761

South Africa
Stephan Phillips (pty) Ltd
Email: orders@stephanphillips.com
Tel: 27 21 4489839 Telefax: 27 21 4479879

Text copyright Shaykh Fadhlalla Haeri 2009

Design: Stuart Davies

ISBN: 978 1 84694 247 1

A CIP catalogue record for this book is available
from the British Library.

Printed by Digital Book Print

O Books operates a distinctive and ethical publishing philosophy in
all areas of its business, from its global network of authors to
production and worldwide distribution.

Happiness in Life and After Death:

An Islamic Sufi View

Shaykh Fadhlalla Haeri

BOOKS

Winchester, UK
Washington, USA

CONTENTS

INTRODUCTION

This book is written for whoever is interested in the Islamic view of life, death and the hereafter. It is based entirely on the Qur'an and the prophetic teachings regarding the purpose and meaning of life on earth and its connection with the eternal Truth. It is written for the present day and relates to our modern knowledge of creation, human needs and the basic path towards a wholesome way of living without forgetting death. Although the emphasis in this book is on death and life after death, matters concerning life on earth and its dynamics and reality are brought to the forefront whenever relevant.

In Islam death is seen as a continuation of life but in an entirely different domain. This life is seen as a preparation for the hereafter, which is beyond the limitations of space and time. My childhood culture made the connection between life and death clearly inseparable. I was born and grew up in the city of Karbala, Iraq, whose fame is derived from the martyrdom of Imam Hussain, the grandson of the Prophet Muhammad. Ever since then it has been a favoured place for burial. Every day thousands of coffins would arrive from far and nearby places to be ceremonially carried for burial in the vast desert necropolis, thereby connecting the life of the living and the dead in practical ways. Remembrance of the dead on weekly and annual bases was an integral part of our life. I grew up imbibing the desire for deeper understanding of the meaning and purpose of life and death. Reflecting about death and preparing for it in practice has made my life richer and deeper. As children we were made to understand that it is through proper understanding of death that we can obtain answers to the questions and challenges that life presents to us. Eternity was thus brought close.

The mystery and certainty of death have made it a perennial human concern, threading through religions, cultures, morality and most other human endeavours, aspirations and fears. Death and dying have preoccupied the human mind and consciousness ever since the dawn of self-awareness. Indeed, fears and concerns about death have distracted us from reflecting upon the key issue of the meaning and purpose of life.

In order to have a positive attitude towards death, we need to look at the nature of birth and the historical background of the origin of life and creation. In our present day, we are endowed with considerable information and knowledge regarding the evolutionary background of all living creatures and human beings. Our lives have been much enriched due to the advancement of science and the popularisation of basic knowledge regarding the nature of light, energy, matter and the magical world of sub atomic particles, as well as astrophysics.

When life becomes perceptibly sentient then the desire for survival and growth follows. In the case of human beings we wilfully desire and seek numerous goals, such as food, procreation, power, rest, company of others, and so on. Death is the end of an individual's interaction with matter/energy, form/meaning and other subject-object dynamics. If there were a form or state of life after death then it could echo, resemble or relate to our life on earth. With death, we lose our worldly senses, mind and perception of space and time and other worldly parameters. 'After-life' implies a zone beyond our normal consciousness and understanding. Hence, it is unknown and this unfamiliarity and uncertainty generates the usual fear and apprehension.

The terms mind consciousness or awareness don't have the exact equivalent in Arabic or in the Qur'an. Islam ascertains that Absolute Truth or God is the only reality from which all other levels of realities, notions and illusions emanate. In Arabic, the term *khayal* refers to the faculty of the imaginal or the illusory, which brings about differentiation and discernment in the world of objects, forms and energies, none of which have an independent or sustainable reality. This most critical human faculty bridges the vast intangible with the discernable world. There is no total independence in our world, as everything in existence has a certain degree of interdependence. Absolute truth alone is independent. Personal identity and 'personality' is reinforced by identification with body, mind and other worldly relationships. The self is a companion shadow of the soul and will only realise relief and contentment after its unity at heart.

> Return to your Lord, well-pleased (with him), well-pleasing (Him), (89:28)

The human soul has emanated from the eternal cosmic soul and is veiled by the illusion of separation as a prelude to returning back to its original source. The various levels of mental states such as intelligence, emotions, feelings, rationality and other elements are all descriptions of different levels of consciousness which have emanated from pure essence or truth, which is in itself free of any qualities or attributes. Illusions and delusions help to maintain a semblance of familiarity and continuity in time and space. Real happiness is the outcome of the realization of the eternal higher consciousness; constant, perfect and blissful. The Qur'an repeatedly describes the friends of God as those who are beyond fear or sorrow.

> Thus whoever believes and acts correctly there will be no fear upon them nor will they grieve. (6:48)

Our so-called 'normal' world works within the realm of causality and the interactions between energy and physical entities. The subatomic world is based on uncertainty. It is no wonder that human beings struggle to realise a state that is always stable, eternal or timeless. It is the realm of higher consciousness that takes us beyond the earthly limitations and enables us to be secure in eternal perfection.

Thus whoever follows my guidance there will be no fear upon them nor will they experience sorrow. (2:38)

Death is the natural door to a higher consciousness where earthly dualities such as good and bad, heavens and earth, the seen and the unseen and objects and subjects are linked and unified. This crossover bridge is a one-way traffic into a new state where we see oneness behind all diverse realities. Our earthly experiences were the nursery of time and space leading to this new realm. For a smooth journey through death to the hereafter, we need to be prepared for a new consciousness without the body, mind, senses, earthly dualities, causality and rationality. Our life on earth is held by boundaries of conditioned consciousness and limitations. Space and time burst forth as a cradle to hold out all that is latent and in potential, before and now, in a discernable and repetitive way, until the cycle returns to where it originated from and by which it is constantly maintained.

Every living entity or conscious creation is endowed with a soul or spirit which acts as the energizing source with its genetic imprints to enable it to grow and evolve towards its maximum potential in performance, intelligence and consciousness. Human beings experience changing and evolving personal consciousness with self awareness and flashes of higher or super consciousness, inspired by the soul within. Other names given to awareness beyond the self are pure consciousness, God awareness, supreme consciousness or higher or absolute consciousness. The more one's personal, specific or conditioned consciousness is aligned with pure consciousness, the deeper, wider and more efficient is the connection with life's essence and source. This act is often referred to as God awareness or remembrance; we often call such a person 'awake', spiritually realised or enlightened. These terms imply synchrony between self-ego and soul, head and heart or created and creator.

...and remember your Lord when you forget and say: "It may be that my Lord guides me unto a nearer way of truth than this." (18:24)

O' you who believe, remember Allah with much remembrance (33:41)

Human beings have access to two spheres of consciousness. The first is primal, conditioned, limited and pervasive in all living entities; it motivates life, survival and other basic evolutionary dynamics. The other dominant sphere carries higher attributes and qualities uniquely accessible to human beings and to a lesser extent some primates, such as generosity, love, patience, justice, compassion, mercy and other subtler qualities desired by human beings. This level of consciousness enables humans to transcend the basic conditioned or egotistic primal consciousness. Spiritual growth entails a smooth connection between these levels of consciousness and reference between self and soul.

The human makeup is both earthly and heavenly, finite and eternal. We experience the physical realm for a short duration, until death ends the illusions of independence and opens the door to the hereafter. When 'coherence' and unity of consciousness is achieved, then life will be experienced as joyful and happy. Thus, the most important issue in human life is to grow from worldly (causal and rational) understanding to higher spiritual wisdom through reference to the light of the soul (or pure consciousness within). The more this higher state is practiced, the less death becomes fearful and it becomes a natural and welcome event in one's personal growth and journey towards timelessness. Limited consciousness returns to the pool of boundlessness from where it emanated. Containment, peace and inner harmony are steps towards seeing universal connectivity and unity; the divine golden thread of universal oneness.

Science and Metaphysics

Modern sciences such as physics, chemistry, mathematics and particularly quantum mechanics provide numerous metaphors and models of what life after death could be like. One example is the dual nature of electrons as a particle and as a wave at the same time. When an electron is intercepted by a screen with two slits, it assumes its wave characteristics and goes through both slits as a wave emerging on the other side with a phenomenon called interference. The patterns of interference are similar to those formed when two stones are thrown into water and the respective ripples subsequently interfere and overlap with each other. When this interference is harmonized, these ripples become 'coherent'. The laser beam's power, and numerous applications in technology, are due to the phenomenon of coherence.

When a person (composed of both body and soul) dies, the soul breaks through the barrier of death emerging as a wave. If during one's lifetime there was synchrony between body, mind, heart and soul, then the process of dying is likely to be easy and natural. Light returns to the realm of lights and matter to matters. Ease and harmony in the afterlife is like coherence and unification.

Until recently scientists kept a good distance from religion and metaphysics, which have lost much of past importance and relevance. Nowadays science is developing its own new form of metaphysics as part of the quest for the grand unifying theory or other attempts to discover the source of what holds the universe together, the physical with the subatomic. What the scientists need is a theory that includes all the forces of nature; the weak and strong forces within the nucleus of the atom, the electromagnetic forces as well as gravity. The string theory is a possible answer to this endeavour. It is perhaps the growing interest in consciousness studies and research that will ultimately shed the needed light onto what connects diverse or different entities and realities. This universal unifying field may also shed new light upon understanding death, dying and the connections between this world and the hereafter.

In the past, human obsession and fear regarding death was answered, for the most part, by religion or other systems of belief or faith. Fear of death and regret for lack of preparation have remained as keynotes throughout human history. In our present day, we have numerous studies of death consciousness through near death experiences (NDEs), as well as out of body experiences (OBEs), meditations and special practices designed to help the mind to transcend so-called normal consciousness.

Until recently, paranormal phenomena (like clairvoyance) were considered spooky and odd. Tests with consciousness-altering drugs and a clearer understanding of brain functions have opened up new channels for better understanding of different levels of consciousness. Our nuclear scientists have been coming up with ideas, theories and models of the quantum world, which are beyond normal human logic or understanding, thus breaking the exclusivity of 'tangible reality' and showing the possibilities of different realms of consciousness. "Schrödinger's Cat" being both dead and alive, at the same time, sounds like the uttering of a mystical hermit who occasionally confuses his devotees with obscure mantras. A century ago such a contradictory idea would have been considered insane. Yet the 'uncertainty principle' is the foundation of our present day quantum physics.

And they say: "O you (Muhammad) to whom the Dhikr (the Qur'an) has been sent down! Verily, you are a mad man." (15:6)

Views of religions and cultures

Historically, many thinkers and philosophers have written about the nature of death and the possibility of an afterlife. Socrates, Plato and Montaigne considered the study of philosophy as essentially the study of death. Michelangelo said, 'No thought exists in me which death has not carved with his chisel.' Awareness of death naturally increases and sharpens human awareness to live fully, with maximum awareness of the present moment and higher consciousness.

Every human being is bound to taste death, [and] in the end unto Us shall all be brought back. (29:57)

As early as the Neanderthals, belief in life-after-death seems evident from drawings and other artefacts recovered from ancient graves and caves. The idea of a new or different kind of consciousness after death can be traced to prehistoric myths and sagas. The Sumerian myth of Gilgamesh, and the great flood of Noah depicted in the Bible and the Qur'an have their echoes in different cultures and religions of the world. Gilgamesh had acquired a rejuvenating plant whose name was 'Old man grown young', which was stolen from him towards the end of his epical journey. As a result, Gilgamesh had to accept that his memorial would be the great walls of the city he had built instead of personal immortality. This is an odyssey of love, labour, hope and a realistic acceptance of the way things are; an ancient example of reconciliation and peaceful surrender to Truth – whatever is born will also die. This perpetual conflict between human love for immortality and the inevitable death of body can only be resolved by realising the soul's ongoingness – light to light and dust to dust.

In Genesis, death is described as the outcome of disobedience to divine commands. In Jewish traditions, the idea of resurrection begins to develop a few centuries B.C. when death was considered to be an act of atonement. Christianity takes some of these Jewish ideas to another level of abstraction and reflects aspects of Zoroastrian notions of destiny beyond death and judgment.

......" Say (O Muhammad): "Who then sent down the Book which Moses brought, a light and a guidance to mankind which you (the Jews), disclosing (some of it) and concealing (much).

And you were taught that which neither you nor your fathers knew." Say: "Allah (sent it down)." Then leave them to play in their vain discussions. (6:91)

Many Eastern religions and cultures consider this world an illusion and therefore promote renunciation and detachment. Life and death are regarded as a natural cycle of an ongoing existence. In these traditions, the history of death is more a history of change in consciousness than a tragedy or liberation. Furthermore, all human experiences are regarded as flawed or as illusions, which veil the truth that can only be revealed through enlightenment. Truth is considered as an absolute and immutable Reality and everything else is a shadow or mirage reflecting this constancy. Nothing is ever as we think it is. Truth gives rise to limited realities and thoughts and is beyond all that is discernible.

To 'see things as they really are' will require the ego and self-identity to transcend to pure consciousness which provides the clear lens through which life can be witnessed. The human self or ego as such is neither bad nor evil – it can be considered a helpful cover over the pure light within the heart until the right time when the self can evolve to realise its soul. The self is a temporary cover shielding the soul and connecting it to the world of change within space and time.

Religious belief in Ancient Egypt was based on the existence of the two different entities—one being the body and the other spirit—and that there would be another physical life after death. Thus, daily life revolved mostly around the concepts of life, death and gods. The Egyptians saw the heart as the source of life and being and that any damage to it would result in a 'second death'. They also had different words for heart. The physical heart was called *Haty*, whilst *Ib* referred to the metaphysical entity embodying thought, intelligence, memory and wisdom, bravery, sadness and love. They believed the deceased went to a territory

9

ruled by *Osiris*, where each person had to give an account of all their good and bad deeds. The idea of death and resurrection stimulated the Egyptian's hope for immortality and produced a code of morality suitable to their culture and way of life.

And you shall see every nation kneeling down; every nation shall be called to its book: today you shall be rewarded for what you did. (45:28)

In Mesopotamia the attitude towards death was very different to that of the Egyptians. The process of death was stark and quite bleak. Sickness was the outcome of sin and wrongdoing, a view that seeped through to the Abrahamic traditions. The death of a person was not connected to any reward in the afterlife; there was no salvation through human effort or divine compassion.

The Jewish literature refers to different kinds of death ranging from the hardest to the easiest. Many allegorical tales discuss the relationship between the living and the dead. It was thought that the dead could communicate with the living, as well as the other way round. The practice of praying for the intercession of the dead was mentioned in the Talmud as part of the custom of visiting the cemetery to request the dead to pray for the living. There are many similarities between Islam and the Old Testament, as well as other Abrahamic teachings.

Those who shall follow the [last] Apostle, the unlettered Prophet whom they shall find described in the Torah that is with them, and [later on] in the Gospel: Those, therefore, who shall believe in him, and honour him, and succour him, and follow the light which is sent down with him: they are the successful ones". (7:157)

Jewish views of the soul begin with the book of Genesis in which verse 2:7 states: 'The lord God formed man from the dust of the earth. He blew into his nostrils the breath of life, and man became a living being.' Although the Hebrew Bible offers no clear definition of the soul, various descriptions of the soul exist in classical

Rabbinical literature. Maimonides, in *The Guide to the Perplexed*, explained classical Rabbinical teaching about the soul through the lens of neo-Aristotelian philosophy. He held that the soul is a person's developed intellect, which has no substance.

The *Zohar*, a classic work of Jewish mysticism (Kabbala), describes the soul as composed of the *Nefesh* (lower part of soul linked to instincts and desires which enter the body at birth), *Ru'ach* and *Neshamah*, developed with action and belief. The first is the lower or animal part of the soul, linked to instincts and bodily cravings. It is found in all humans and enters the body at birth and it is the source of one's physical and psychological nature. The other two parts of the soul are said to only fully exist in people of awakened spirituality. *Ru'ach* (the middle soul) contains the moral virtues and the ability to distinguish between good and evil. *Nashamah* (the higher soul) is what separates man from all other forms of life and is related to the intellect, which allows man to enjoy and benefit from the afterlife.

> They said: O our people! We have listened to a Book revealed after Moses verifying that which is before it, guiding to the truth and to a right path: (46:30)

In the Kabbalistic teachings, many of the key terms used have similar counterparts in Arabic. The *Nefesh* (nafs: breath and/or soul) disintegrates after death and the *Ru'ach* (ruh: soul) is sent to a sort of intermediate zone where it is submitted to purification and enters 'temporary paradise'. Whilst *Neshamah* returns to the source and enjoys the 'kiss of the beloved' supposedly after resurrection, *Ru'ach* and *Neshamah* are united again in a permanently trans-muted state of being.

Other Kabbalistic works state that there are two more parts of the human soul, which are considered to represent the most sublime levels of intuitive cognition and to be within the grasp of only a few chosen individuals. This aspect is considered as part of the soul that allows one to have an awareness of the Divine presence. The other part is the highest plane of the soul in which one can achieve as close a union with God as is possible.

> And before this was the Book of Moses as a guide and a mercy. And this is a confirming Book (the Qur'an) in the Arabic language, to warn those who do wrong, and as glad tidings to the good-doers (46:12)

Most Christians believe the soul (or spirit) to be the immortal essence of a human and that after death the soul is either rewarded or punished. Whether this reward is contingent upon good deeds or merely upon belief in God, the father, and Jesus, the son, is a constant debate among different Christian groups.

In Christianity the eschatological concepts deal with the last 'four things': death, judgment, heaven and hell. Death is simply considered separation between body and soul and is the consequence and penalty of Adam's original sin. It is the end event of man's period of probation and decides his eternal destiny. We will not all sleep, but we will all be changed' (1: Cor 15:51); 'Dust you are, and unto dust shall you return' (Gen 3:19); 'Earth to earth, ashes to ashes, dust to dust; in sure and certain hope of resurrection' (The Common Book of Prayers).

> And do not argue with the followers of the Book (other revealed religions) except by what is best, and say: We believe in what has been revealed to us and revealed to you, and our God and your God is One, and to Him do we submit. (29:46)

Within Christianity the idea of purgatory is based on the premise that the soul, if imperfect, spends a period purging or cleansing before being ready for the end of time. Purgatory is the intermediate state of unknown duration relevant to the extent of sins and missed repentance. They undergo a course of penal purification in order to be admitted into heaven. They share in the communion of the saints, and benefit by the prayer and good works of the living.

> And indeed, We gave Moses the Book and followed him up with a succession of Messengers... (2:87)

In Christian theology, heaven is the abode of the blessed where they will be elevated by the light of glory so as to be capable of enjoying the company of Christ and the angels and the immediate vision of God, face to face. Only the perfectly pure and holy enter heaven. There are some who have attained that state at death, while others enter heaven after a course of purification and purgatory, without much delay. Hell designates the place or state of men and angels who are excluded from beatific vision due to their sins.

In the early centuries of Christianity, the Gnostic Valentinus proposed a version of spiritual psychology that was in accordance with numerous other perennial doctrines. He conceived of human beings as a triple entity, consisting of body (*hyle*), soul (*psyche*), and spirit (*pneuma*). This is identical to the division found in St Paul's epistle to Thessalonians I.

> And when Allah said: O Jesus, I shall cause you death and cause you to ascend unto Me and purify you of those who disbelieve and make those who follow you above those who disbelieve to the day of resurrection; then to Me shall be your return, so I will judge between you in the matters in which you used to dispute. (3:55)

The idea of a spiritual essence for mankind is well described in Islam (especially Sufism) and echoed in several world religions such as Buddhism, Vedanta and others. In modern transpersonal psychologies it is known as the soul-spark or higher self.

According to Buddhist teachings, all things are impermanent and in a constant state of flux. All is transient and there is no abiding state. This is applied to humanity as much as anything else in the cosmos. Thus, there is no unchanging self. Our sense of 'I' or 'me' is simply a sense of belonging to the ever-changing entity composed of body and mind.

Buddhists hold that the delusion of a permanent self is one of the main roots of human conflict on the emotional, social and political levels. It is through understanding the 'not-self' that we gain insight into the human condition, which allows us to go beyond 'our' mundane desires. At death the body and mind disintegrate; any remaining traces of *karma* will cause the continuity of consciousness to bounce back as thought in the future mind of a foetus. Some Buddhist teachers, however, affirm that although permanent personal selfhood is denied, concepts such as Buddha-nature or original nature are valid. They take the view that if there is no abiding self and no soul then there is no cause to be reborn.

Say to (them): "If the home of the Hereafter with Allah is indeed for you specially and not for others, of mankind, then long for death if you are truthful." (2:94)

The Tibetan Buddhist *Book of the Dead* gives guidance for the stages during the process of dying and the 'Bardo' realm, or intermediate state, following death, prior to the next rebirth. Death for the Buddhist occurs on different levels and in different stages. Life and death are considered integral elements of one great cycle within the continuation and flowering of life. It is considered that the last thoughts before death are most important and we need to guard against inappropriate habitual thoughts throughout our life. Last thoughts are naturally related to the usual regular patterns of thinking and one's general inner state.

In Hinduism, the Sanskrit word most closely corresponding to the soul is *Atman*, which can mean soul or even God. It is seen as

14

the portion of *Brahman* (God) within us. Hinduism contains many variant beliefs on the origin, purpose and fate of the soul. For example, *Advaita* or the non-dualistic conception of the soul, accords its union with Brahman, the absolute uncreated. *Davaita*, or dualistic concepts, identify the soul as a different and incompatible substance.

Jainists believe in a *Jiva*, an immortal essence of a living being analogous to a soul, which is subject to the illusion of *maya* and evolves through many incarnations from mineral to vegetable to animal. Its accumulated *karma* determines the form of its next birth.

Islamic View of Death

According to Islam, death is not the end of life but a transformation from this world to the hereafter. Life after death is called *akhira* or that which comes later or lasting. It is a transition from earthly transitory experiences to a higher, clearer and subtler lasting life. It is a transition from a constrained and insecure state of life to a new horizon of pure consciousness. Human beings will simply shift from one place or state to another. Death is a bridge, taking the pious believers from worldly changes, hardships and afflictions to the widely spread gardens and permanent blessings of afterlife. After the limited life span in this world, death will lead to a new start of the boundless beyond space/time. The Qur'an and Prophetic traditions tell us that only the physical body, senses and ego will taste death and not the soul or essence within the heart.

> And who believe in that which has been revealed to you and that which was revealed before you and they are sure of the hereafter. (2:4)

Death will cause the physical body to perish—sense and personal will suspended—but the soul with its attending shadow of a person's balance sheet of good and bad actions and intentions carry on to the hereafter. The Prophet taught that human beings have been created for the next permanent realm and not for this temporary and deceptive world. He emphasised that man was created for permanent happiness and not fleeting happiness. Our earthly life is but a preparation and passage towards the next world. The three phases of human growth start with the darkness of the womb and then comes the changing lights and shadows of this world, leading to the clearer lights of the hereafter. Experientially, we know that permanent happiness is not attainable in this world and yet we cannot stop pursuing it. The self is restless to attain its soul.

The Prophet Muhammad said: 'Death is a gift for the believer, like a pleasant fragrance; more deaths occur due to people's sins than to the stipulated time, and people live longer due to their good deeds than their determined life span.' The implication is that our intentions, thoughts and actions have a big part to play in our destiny. Every situation describes its ultimate destiny.

............Say: "Short is the enjoyment of this world. The Hereafter is (far) better for him who fears Allah, and you shall not be dealt with unjustly even minutely." (4:77)

Islam describes two types of death: physical and spiritual. Those who do not respond to the call and message of Allah are considered as 'dead' (in this world) in the eyes of Allah. The Qur'an states:

Surely you do not make the dead to hear, and you do not make the deaf to hear the call when they go back retreating. (27:80)

Is he, who was dead (ignorant) and We gave him life (knowledge) and set for him a light (of Belief) whereby he can walk amongst men, like him who is in the darkness from which he can never come out? Thus it is made fair seeming (pleasing) to the disbelievers that which they used to do. (6:122)

The Prophet taught that worldly people think that 'physical death' of a person is a major event, but the righteous consider spiritual death as greater and more grievous. Islam condones death for the sake of Allah, Truth and Justice, and those who die as such are considered ever living. The Qur'an states:

And say not of those who are slain in God's cause, "They are dead": nay, they are alive, but you perceive it not. (2:154)

He who emigrates (from his home) in the Cause of Allah, will find on earth many dwelling places and plenty to live by. And whosoever leaves his home as an emigrant unto Allah and His Messenger, and death overtakes him, his reward is then surely incumbent upon Allah. And Allah is Ever Oft-Forgiving, Most Merciful. (4:100)

Dying for the cause of truth does not mean only on battlefields and in physical struggles, which are termed 'lesser jihad'. To go against one's ego and selfish desires, greed, love of power and dominance, is considered a greater battle or jihad and can therefore be considered as a sacrifice (death of ego) for the sake of truth and enlightenment. The key issue is to be willing to give up what is considered valuable or important, in a worldly sense, for the sake of purification of heart and light and God's pleasure or command.

The Qur'an also mentions two different times of death: a definite time (fixed destiny) and an indefinite or changeable time as described in the verses.

It is He, Who takes your souls by night (in sleep), and has knowledge of all that you have done by day, then he raises (wakes) you up again that a term appointed (your life period) be fulfilled, then in the end unto Him will be your return. Then He will inform you what you used to do. (6:60)

And (commanding you): "Seek the forgiveness of your Lord, and turn to Him in repentance, that He may grant you good enjoyment, for a term appointed…" (11:3).

Whoever hopes for the Meeting with Allah, then Allah's Term is surely coming. And He is the All-Hearer, the All-Knower. (29:5).

Sleep is considered a type of temporary death. Natural or normal death is different to accidental and untimely death, which often comes suddenly and as a shock.

Islam does not uphold the soul's reincarnation or transmutation as such, although there are a few descriptions in the Qur'an which some commentators view as exceptional examples of a soul's return to the earthly realms.

The Qur'an also states that nations and civilizations also follow a course of maturity and then an inevitable decline and disintegration. As cited earlier:

And every nation has its appointed term; when their term is reached, neither can they delay it an hour nor can they advance it. (7:34)

According to the Qur'an, when a group of people or nation becomes 'oppressor' and 'tormentor', Allah will hasten their end:

And every nation has its appointed term; when their term is reached, neither can they delay it an hour nor can they advance it.) – (And how many of the generations did We destroy after Nuh! and your Lord is sufficient as Knowing and Seeing with regard to His servants' faults. (17:16-17)

The Qur'an emphasises lack of foreknowledge of the place or time of death:

... and no one knows in what land he will die. Verily, God [alone] is all-knowing, all-aware. (31:34)

The implication is perpetual cautious awareness of thoughts and actions and accountability at all times in order to remain mentally prepared for death at any place or time. Whoever remembers death frequently is more likely to live at a higher level of awareness of intentions, actions and consciousness.

The Qur'an describes the angels who execute God's decrees as agents connecting the world of senses with the intangible domain.

Or do they think that we do not hear what they conceal and their secret discourses? Yes! And our messengers (angels) are with them recording. (43:80)

Angels carry out numerous duties and activities, affecting life on earth. Some angels are known as the generous scribes (*kiramin katibin*). One is deputed to record bad deeds and thoughts (on the left) whilst the other records good intentions and thoughts (on the right hand side). Then there are angels of death who have been assigned to take away the souls of people, of whom the archangel of death (Izra'il) is their chief.

Say: The angel of death who is given charge of you shall cause you to die, then to your Lord you shall be brought back. (32:11)

The Prophet Muhammad was present at the deathbed of a man when he saw the Angel of Death near him. He told the angel to be kind to the dying man and the archangel replied, 'Be sure that I am kind to the believers and that I pull out the soul of people (only as destined). By God, we don't wrong any person; we do not take the soul earlier or later than the appointed time. If a person accepts the will of God, he will depart with ease and if he objects with resentment and grief, he will be punished for it. '

After the world is destroyed and every living entity has gone through death, Izra'il, Jibra'il, Mika'il and the other angels bearing the throne of Allah will still be alive. Then Allah will order the death of Jibra'il and Mika'il. Then comes the death of the bearers of the throne. Finally, the archangel of death (Izra'il) will also die. The Prophet Muhammad said, 'On the Day of Judgment, Allah will make the angel of death taste death as all of his other servants.'

From the Qur'an and other Prophetic Traditions, it can be surmised that the balance of a person's deeds and intentions in this world will be carried forward to the hereafter. Power, wealth, offspring, prestige and other worldly desirables are of no consequence then. It is only what has been done for the good of others and in the way of charity, justice and truth, which will have a lasting effect in the after-world. Whatever helps to purify the heart and lighten the burden of the soul is considered good and helpful. Ultimately, it is witnessing creation through the light of unity that will liberate one from darkness. Shirk, or seeing other than the One, is at the root of all injustices, double standards, hypocrisy and confusion on earth.

> Surely, God does not forgive shirk (associating others with Him) although He forgives what is beside that. (4:48)

> Unto God belongs all that is in the heavens and all that is on earth. And whether you bring into the open what is in your minds or conceal it, God will call you to account for it; and then He will forgive whom He wills, and will chastise whom He wills: for God has the power to will anything. (2:284)

The sequences and order of events towards the end of time or doomsday do not follow a clear time line which corresponds to what our minds comprehend in this world of space and time. Understandably, these future events take place in a domain where time is no longer operative as on earth. In the Qur'an, hell and paradise are mentioned numerous times but these experiences are not slotted neatly in stages after death and resurrection but are diffused and interlinked throughout the hereafter as well as life on earth. In other words, difficulty or ease begins with birth and continue after death according to personal thoughts and actions. Hell or paradise does not begin only after receiving the account after doomsday. The Prophet had said that a person's grave is either part of paradise or hell, i.e. according to his deeds and inner state. The Qur'an states:

O people! If you are in doubt about the Resurrection, then verily! We have created you from dust, then from a sperm then from a clot then from a little lump of flesh, some formed and some unformed, that We may make (it) clear to you. And We cause whom We will to remain in the wombs for an appointed term, then We bring you out as infants, then that you may reach your age of full strength. And among you there is he who dies (young), and among you there is he who is brought back to the feeblest old age, so that he knows nothing after having known. And you see the earth barren, but when We send down water (rain) on it, it is stirred (to life), it swells and puts forth every lovely kind (of growth) – (That is because Allah, He is the Truth, and it is He Who gives life to the dead, and it is He Who is Able to do all things.) (22:5-6)

Was he not once a [mere] drop of sperm that had been spilt, and thereafter became a germ-cell - whereupon He created and formed [it] in accordance with what [it] was meant to be, and fashioned out of it the two sexes, the male and the female? Is not He, then; able to bring the dead back to life? (75:37-40)

Life on earth is echoed in the hereafter. Everything in creation is part of a chain of events and is one of two pairs of entities which can be similar or different.

We create man out of the essence of clay, and then We cause him to remain as a drop of sperm in [the wombs] firm keeping, and then We create out of the drop of sperm a germ-cell, and then We create out of the germ-cell an embryonic lump, and then We create within the embryonic lump bones, and then We clothe the bones with flesh – and then We bring [all] this into being as a new creation: And then, behold! After all this, you are destined to die; and then, behold! You shall be raised from the dead on Resurrection Day. (23:12-16)

And that it is He who creates the two kinds - the male and the female – out of a [mere] drop of sperm as it is poured forth, and that [therefore] it is within His power to bring about a second life. (53:45-47)

The origin and metaphor of fire (and hell) is mentioned several times in the Qur'an with regards to resurrection,

Say: "He who brought them into being in the first instance will give them life [once again], seeing that He has full knowledge of every act of creation: He who produces for you fire out of the green tree, so that, lo! you kindle [your fires] therewith." (36:79-80)

Have you ever considered the fire which you kindle? Is it you who have produced its tree (origin) - or are We the cause of its coming into being? We have made it a Reminder and an article of use for the journey." (56:71-73)

Signs and events of doomsday have been mentioned in numerous prophetic traditions. These include depression of the earth in the East and the earth bursting open in the West; smoke filling the skies; the earth splitting open in the Arabian Peninsula; *Dajjal* (the impostor) and other beasts will appear from under the earth; *Gog* and *Magog* (barbaric tribes) will appear and assault the people; the sun will rise from the West; Jesus will reappear and storms will blow and drown people in the sea. These and other catastrophic events herald the great assembly of creation. The last three chapters in this book present the Qur'anic description of doomsday and the human state of peace and ease or difficulty and affliction, which starts from the moment of death and continues further until resurrection and the end of time.

'Signs of the Hour' are often quoted by traditional Muslim preachers and scholars as well as 'end-of-timers', who emphasise the imminence of the end of time. For centuries, Muslims have often interpreted the moral ills and weaknesses of their societies as an indication of the nearness of the time of Judgement. 'Last day' literature often appears in parallel with the 'time of *Mahdi*', the awaited messiah, especially during difficult times, social upheavals and crises. The rising of the sun in the west, contrary as it is to its usual course in nature, is interpreted in recent times by some Muslim populists as a reference to the rising power of western nations. These obscurants regard this as a demonstration of God's anger (against the West) for He favours the Middle East from where most of the prophets emerged! The regularity of antici-pating the 'last day' has become a historical fact which appeals to the general believing public and especially the poorer and less educated people. No century goes by without the rise and fall of numerous self-declared 'Mahdis' or 'messiahs' in the Muslim world.

The Prophet Muhammad often emphasised the importance of remembrance of death and being prepared for it at all times. 'Die before you die' is a frequently quoted tradition. The general meaning of this teaching is to be ready to leave this world in submission to the will of the generous and just God with ease and peace of mind. This state is attained by having the least amount of attachments to, and love of, worldly belongings and relationships. A deeper meaning is to let the lower consciousness die ('lower life' is often quoted in the Qur'an) and to live for and by the higher ('other', 'later' or 'lasting' life), which relates to God consciousness. These teachings and Qur'anic verses become transformative when one reflects and meditates upon the purpose and meaning of life and the human freedom and responsibility. Islam is the path of grooming the lower self and purifying the heart and unifying the self and soul. This spiritual evolvement will lift the individual consciousness out of the ever-changing worldly uncertainties to the domain of insights and inner delights. Whatever we love in this world we shall lose, except the sacred soul which lives on.

In this brief book, I have attempted to connect historical, religious and cultural ideas of Islam regarding the nature of death with contemporary interpretations and understanding. The Prophetic Teaching and the Qur'an emphasise the view that birth and death are natural cycles in the journey of the human soul back to its original divine source – Allah who is omnipresent. Life on earth is a metaphor for life after death and everything we experience here is a sample of what exists in the unseen as energy patterns or archetypes. Our life on earth is ever connected to our next life and is the preparation for it. The connection between life and death is natural and understandable by reason, faith, contemplation and insights. The human tendency to search for genealogical roots, or connection with dead ancestors, is an echo of the self's search for its soul (the life source) and our higher sacred origin. The restless and insecure self or ego is searching for its source of life, which is the soul within the human heart.

It is He Who gives life, and causes death, and to Him you (all) shall return. (10:56)

At the end of each chapter, I have appended some additional relevant selections of Qur'anic Verses and Prophetic teachings which are well known (with some linguistic variation) amongst Muslims. I request the reader to reflect on the golden thread that binds these chapters together. When we connect any specific experience or awareness to a higher level of consciousness we are on the path of spiritual evolution from the specific and relative to the higher and absolute. Physical death is the natural prelude to the soul's liberation and flight to the domain of boundlessness, perfection and goodness of the eternal oneness – God.

Allah does not call you to account for what is vain in your oaths, but He will call you to account for what your hearts have earned, and Allah is Forgiving, Forbearing. (2:225)

LIGHTS AND SHADOWS

It is normal that human life leads consciousness to widen, deepen and evolve towards higher consciousness and wisdom. This chapter examines several facets that are involved in the development of consciousness and the interplay of countless dualities, light and shadows, self and soul and the different spheres of consciousness. Conditioned consciousness relates to the sentiency and self-awareness of individuals and the urge for survival and growth. Higher level of consciousness relates to the soul (or spirit) and the realm of boundlessness. These two spheres meet within the human heart which creates the experience of oneness of the authentic self, even though changes are occurring all the time. This unified field becomes fully integrated when self and soul are in synchrony and the person's state of mind and behaviour are in harmony.

Light

All praise is due to Allah, Who created the heavens and the earth and made the darkness and the light; yet those who disbelieve set up equals with their Lord. (6:1)

The essence, origin and structure of life is often explained by the notion of light. The Qur'an describes God's principal attribute as light by declaring Allah as the Light (essence) of heavens and earth. In Arabic, the words light and fire (*noor* and *nar*) are derived from the same root, implying that paradise and hell emanate from the same One source: the eternal cosmic Light. All creations draw their energy and life from this ever-present Light and, as such, they are flickering shadows with beginnings and ends or birth and death, proving the existence of the eternal divine Light. Hence, all life emanates from this sacred Light, sustained by it and returns to it. Fire consumes matter and 'purifies' it to produce light!

Allah is the guardian of those who believe. He brings them out of the darkness into the light; and (as to) those who disbelieve, their guardians are Shaitans who take them out of the light into the darkness; they are the inmates of the fire, in it they shall abide. (2:257)

It is He who grants life and deals death; and when He wills a thing to be, He just says to it, 'Be!', and it is. (40:68)

1.2 Spheres of Consciousness

The experience of the numerous facets of human consciousness is perhaps one of life's greatest mysteries. Awareness of consciousness is a condition that distinguishes us from all other animals. Human self-awareness implies two spheres of consciousnesses: the first is local, limited, conditioned and evolving personal consciousness. The second sphere is of a higher level – the pure and supreme source and essence of the universe. The latter is like electric power giving rise to the former (as a fan, light bulb or a pump). Conditioned consciousness radiates from the soul to energise the body, the mind and the intellect, whilst higher consciousness is a subtle light force emanating from God – the cosmic soul. When conditioned consciousness leads to pure consciousness, intelligence, discernment and differentiation leads to insights, wisdom and illumination. This state is the purpose of all human endeavours, which can be experienced in this life or after death.

On that day Allah will pay back to them in full their just reward, and they shall know that Allah is the evident Truth. (24:25)

Human consciousness is the root and origin of our ability to discern different entities, qualities, quantities and dualities which interact, complement and connect with each other. All human action is motivated by the desire to attract something or repel something else. The human mind realises that some aspects of this life are physical and material, whilst others are more subtle at the levels of feeling or intuition. We also differentiate between that which is inner or hidden and that which is outer or obvious. It is common to constantly review and change what is considered good or bad, what is valuable or worthless and what action is generous or mean, friendly or hostile and what is personal and what concerns society. Context and appropriateness in thought and action are the foundation of wisdom and insights. Consciousness arises with self-awareness and concern for personal survival and welfare. It evolves towards higher levels.

> That He may pay them back fully their rewards and give them more out of His grace: surely He is Forgiving, most ready to appreciate good deeds. (35:30)

It is natural that as we mature and evolve we increase our knowledge and skills in personal performance and in relationships. The drive for excellence is due to the pull of higher consciousness. God's perfection draws everything in creation towards it. The natural boundaries between one's self and others become blurred with increased understanding, sympathy, empathy, depth and breadth of perception and insight into human nature and its composition. Through wisdom we witness greater and deeper interconnectedness and relationships between creations and their source and between self and soul. We realise that, every living entity has a soul which is energised by the first primal source. Thus, there is a unity underlying all visible diversities.

> Is someone who was dead (without Faith or knowledge) and whom we brought to life (by knowledge and faith) supplying him with a light (of guidance) by which to walk among people, the same as someone who is in utter darkness (ignorance),

unable to emerge from it? Thus to those without faith their own deeds seem pleasing. (6:122)

Whatever we experience in creation relates to different fields of energy or patterns, which are woven in multidimensional ways within a unified field of universal Oneness. This is God's power, will and light. This unifying field is the supreme consciousness to which all of creation is connected and is the cause of the drive of self and soul to unite. If a person is not fully unified and attained inner integration or realises eternal oneness, then unity and harmony remains an elusive idea. All of our experiences and insights oscillate between oneness and countless dualities. One essence, source or truth gives rise to the universal diversities and short-lived entities.

> Say: Who is the Lord of the heavens and the earth? Say: Allah. Say: So why have you taken protectors apart from Him who possess no power to help or harm themselves? Are the blind and the seeing alike? Or can the darkness and the light be equal? Or have they assigned partners to Allah who create as He creates, so that all creating seems the same to them? Say: Allah is the Creator of all things, and He is the One, the Irresistible. (13:16)

Human beings are the middle kingdom or isthmus between the seen and unseen, heavens and earth, the absolute and relative and limited and cosmic-consciousness. The human soul is like a hologram replicating the cosmic soul. The Qur'an describes God as the Light of heavens and earth and the parable of that Light is the light within the breast of humankind. Everything else is like a shadow that is discernable due to this light. The Qur'an also refers to the colours of God, which are the divine attributes etched within the soul. It describes the soul as being from the breath of the Lord and that it carries on to the next world after

29

the death of the body.

> Our messenger has come to you making clear to you much of the Book that you have kept concealed and forgiving much; indeed, there has come to you light and a clear Book from Allah; (5.15).

> By it (the Book) Allah guides those who follow what pleases Him to the ways of peace. He will bring them from the darkness to the light by His permission and guide them to a straight path (5:16)

1.3 The Purpose of Life

The real challenge is to understand that the human microcosm — which contains everything that can be known, experienced or sensed — is a reflection and mirror of the macrocosm. The ultimate purpose of life is to experience and realise synchronicity between these two complementary states and thus attain unity. The source of all knowledge is already within the human heart and the spiritual path connects mind, heart, self and soul. The Prophet had commanded; "Cut down your worldly desires, it will remove your (inner) poverty; and cut down your sins, it will make the death (detachment) easy." He had also said, "Know that you have been created for the next lasting world, and not for this world of destruction and death. You are in a place that does not belong to you, and you are chased by death, which would surely overtake everyone."

To be a friend of God and reliant on the sacred light is considered the ultimate in life's purpose and attainment. This state of transcendence brings about joy and is beyond fear or sorrow. Rivalry, jealousy, competitiveness and desire to be "number one" are echoes of the self or ego desiring to be like the soul – perfect, eternal and in bliss.

Now surely the friends of Allah – will feel no fear and know no sorrow (10.62).

1.4 Matter and Energy

Matter and energy interactions in creation produce all that appear and disappear, begin and end, with all other changing characteristics. The natural relationship and interchange between everything in creation (matter or form) and its energy state is fundamental to our world. The pool of energy in existence is constant and that matter is a form of energy appearing in physical form for a while. Eventually the energy available for work will be lost as heat resulting in the thermal death of the universe and its return to the realm of pre-creation. Modern school physics nowadays teaches that the atom is not a fixed or solid material entity. All the constituent parts of the atom are energy entities with vast spaces between them. Quantum physics has eroded the old cosy model of 'material' atoms being the building blocks of our physical world. Science had proved that subatomic entities are composed of energies that behave in ways not logical or predictable by our normal human measures or understanding. Like the nature of the hereafter, it doesn't follow our everyday logic.

The relationship between what is considered tangible and real and that which is intangible and uncertain is subtle and follows dynamic exchanges at the quantum level. Energy is potential matter and every physical entity or form is on its way to being released as energy. The Qur'an repeatedly declares that whatever is in the heavens or earth is held and permeated by the One God, who is simultaneously evident as well as hidden.

He is the First and the Last, and the Outward and the Inward; and He has Knowledge of all things. (57:3)

No calamity can happen in the earth or in your selves unless it is recorded in a decree before existence. (57: 22)

Do they not see the birds, suspended in mid air in the sky? Nothing holds them there except for the power of Allah. There are certainly signs in that for people who believe. (16:79)

The photon is both a package of light as well as a wave affecting every aspect of this life that appears and disappears, discernible on some occasions and unseen at others. Consciousness may be subtler and faster than light and its subtler levels can only be subjectively experienced by human beings, who can transcend the conditioned personal state of consciousness to higher levels. The Qur'an gives several examples of how time is relative and space is deceptive, in that it can be traversed in an instant as happened with the Prophetic Journey or ascent to the heavens (*mi'raj*).

Do you not see that Allah has subjected to your (use) all things in the heavens and on earth, and has made His bounties flow to you in exceeding measure, (both) seen and unseen? Yet there are people who argue about Allah, without knowledge or guidance or without a Book to enlighten them. (31:20).

Also, the Qur'an describes a day with God is like a thousand years on earth. Or that the day, or periods, with angels is like fifty thousand years. Time is simply relative.

And a day with your hand is like a thousand years as you count. (22:47)

The angels and the spirit ascend to Him in a day whose length is fifty thousand years. (70:4)

Like many other realities, matter and energy appear with different characteristics whilst they are interrelated and inseparable. We human beings contain both. We are composed of matter, which can remain sentient by converting food into energy. We also have an unseen essence, which is the source of life in us and which we call soul or spirit. We encompass the subatomic entities as well as the astrophysical states of immense spaces and energy sources confirming the description of 'middle people'. We are both heavenly and earthly at the same time but can discern one or the other state at any one instant.

> In this way we have made you a middlemost (just) community so that you may act as witnesses against mankind, and that the Messenger (act) as a witness against you. We only appointed the direction you used to face (direction of qiblah) in order to distinguish those who follow the Messenger from those who turn round on their heels, though in truth it is a very hard thing except for those whom Allah has guided. Allah would never let your faith go to waste; Allah is All Gentle, Most Merciful to people. (2:143)

1.5 Origin of Creation

The Qur'an describes the original void or the state before creation as a seamless and non-differentiated or discernible realm. Dispersion then occurred from this original cosmic 'dense' oneness or gatheredness. This is the start of the so-called big bang. That same so-called void or cosmic soul exists throughout what we experience as worldly realities. All apparent creations are sustained by one universal unique reality – God. Only Allah was, is and will forever be. In truth, there is none in existence except the One and only God or cosmic soul. Creation is a result of divine effulgence and grace, which was before space and time and permeates everything within all of space and time.

> Do those who are disbelievers not see that the heavens and the earth were joined together (inseparable), then We parted them?

And We have made from water every living thing. Will they not then believe? (21:30)

Space/time is the nursery where consciousness provides the soil, air, water and sun for the seed of selfhood with its mind and intellect to grow, evolve and reach the higher consciousness of the soul. From the One, by the One, and unto the One. Truth has always been one and absolute and from it emanates infinite varieties of relative entities, realities and energies. Every creation seeks to realise its original root and oneness through the maze of multiplicities and complementary opposites. Grieving or rejoicing, winning or losing, are all natural outcomes of the self's quest for the ultimate joy of being one with the soul.

(Allah) The Most Beneficent: It is He Who taught the Qur'an. He created man: He taught him eloquent speech. (55:1-4)

Qur'an is the source book which contains all the signs and symbols of how countless varieties of creations emanate and return to the One essence, which permeates all perpetually.

One way of looking at this model is to think of a cosmic soul giving rise to countless mineral, vegetable, animal and human souls, each with limitations and potentials. Souls within each category resonate with each other and as such know and reflect each other, even though sensations and perceptions (at any period of time) are different. It is like pure light giving rise to countless colours and hues echoing their origin. This is the meaning of the saying that there are as many ways to God as there are human beings. The child sees everyone as different; the wise one sees everyone as the same. One looks at the outer, the other perceives the inner.

Often religions and philosophy are concerned with how to reconcile life, death and the hereafter with the idea of divine mercy, grace and compassion. How does eternal truth or the absolute relate to the ever-changing, relative manifestations; how does one see the sublime in ridiculous appearances, discern order within chaos, or good within bad, or see death as an aspect of life and complementary to birth.

> Look then at the signs of Allah's mercy, how He gives life to the earth after its death, most surely He will raise the dead to life; and He has power over all things. (30:50)

God, or supreme consciousness, is what connects all levels of subtle and gross fields and states, which emanate from it and return to it. The Qur'an states that 'everything in creation is in adoration (worshipping) of God'. The act of worship implies love, knowledge and the passionate desire to be at one with this glorious all-encompassing Essence.

> Allah is He to whom the kingdom of the heavens and the earth belongs. He gives life and causes to die. You have no protector or helper besides Allah. (9:116)

REFLECTIVE CONSCIOUSNESS

Our worldly experiences are preludes to the next zone of consciousness after death. This idea or paradigm will help us to go through life with greater ease and grace. It is not enough to be limited to conditioned consciousness and self-interest. There is always a natural quest for the higher, subtler and more enduring state of consciousness. Biological evolution and personal consciousness are necessary starting points towards higher consciousness, spiritual evolution and greater inner stability, contentment and wisdom. An awakened person connects material, mental, emotional and spiritual issues and sees the world from a unified viewpoint. One's life experiences are conditioned by the inner state.

And that man will have nothing except what he does [good or bad]. (53:39)

2.1 Love of Divine Qualities

Biological evolution and natural selection are energised by conditioned consciousness. The drive for higher consciousness and spiritual awakening follows. Every human being grows and evolves towards its higher potential. By the mysterious farce of creation, we have evolved from one cell over many millions of years; then there were plants which grew, drawing nourishment out of insentient minerals. All minerals replicate themselves (as in crystal growth) and form clusters according to natural laws. Plants and other living creatures, especially animals, follow a pattern of natural selection towards a more durable state and greater sense of awareness. Naturally, the outer world and its changing conditions have a significant influence on the specific as well as the general state of creations.

We created mankind out of dried clay (like pottery that makes sound), from black mud moulded in shape. (15:26)

When I have formed him and breathed (some of) my Spirit into him, fall down (you angels) in prostration in front of him! (15:29)

For every living person, the inner state and the outer environment are constantly reflecting each other, giving rise to either agreeable attraction or repulsion and disintegration. Every living entity aspires to higher consciousness and the qualities associated with it, such as knowledge, power and constancy. The Qur'an declares that whatever is contained in the Heavens and Earth glorifies God (His qualities). Human beings are created in love with God's attributes and perfections as depicted in our souls. The fall of Adam (personalised consciousness) was necessary for the struggle to ascend back to higher consciousness which symbolizes the awakened state as well as the stewardship of man on earth. We all desire wellbeingness, excellence and perfection in all endeavours.

Human souls are, in essence, heavenly and boundless. Thus, we all struggle to be relieved from the limitations of physicality. We draw life and energy from supreme consciousness via our souls. We are souls with bodies and minds as appendages. Each human soul contains qualities and imprints which reflect aspects of the cosmic soul or God. Whilst souls of different creations have varying limitations and every soul reproduces some aspect of the higher attributes that it possesses. For example, 'the Ever-Living' quality of God is reflected by all sentient creatures as the essential drive to survive, live on and grow. Human beings aspire to the higher qualities of mercy, generosity, beauty, love and other such attributes due to higher consciousness and passion for God's qualities and beautiful names.

O man! Surely, you must strive (to attain) to your Lord, a hard striving until you meet Him. (84:6)

2.2 Potential Human Consciousness

Whatever that can exist is ever-present. God's light permeates heavens and earth and thus sustains the universe and all of creation therein – known and unknown. Every living entity is defined by its soul's consciousness and aspires to its highest possible level. Only the human being can transcend the limited personal conditioned consciousness to God consciousness. Paranormal phenomena, clairvoyance and other psychic states are due to transcending ego consciousness to the soul and higher states through prayers, meditation, trance and other means. There, unusual phenomena occur due to accessing the energy bands and fields of subtle universal connections that are close by. This is how flashes of the past, future or present knowledge are revealed to prophetic beings, seers, sages and others. When the self is aligned to soul consciousness and the mind is still and free of thought, then one is engulfed by higher consciousness and the field of cosmic oneness.

And He taught Adam all the names (Divine attributes and knowledges)… (2:31)

Names relate to all aspects of knowledge and higher qualities and attributes, which are like energy fields within higher consciousness. The balanced and healthy human state draws energy from both spheres of consciousness (conditioned-personal and higher) simultaneously. For survival, we need the basic, personal or conditioned consciousness. Higher consciousness opens up doors to insights and sublime qualities that connect the seen and the unseen, within space/time and beyond, life on earth and the hereafter. The human being is designed to be on the "middle path" between seen and unseen, the lowest and highest states; between earth and heavens.

Our so-called 'real world' is discerned through a spectrum of consciousnesses. The outer world of physical entities and creations is subject to all the natural laws of biology, physics, chemistry and other regulations. The subtle, subatomic or quantum world is the foundation of the material world with its own logic and laws which are radical and unique. The logic of the inner workings of atoms or molecules and their dynamics seem most illogical to our minds, for the usual laws of the physical world do not apply at the small particle level.

> When your Lord said to the angels: I am going to put a viceroy on the earth, they said: "Why put on it (the earth) one who will cause corruption and shed blood, when we glorify you and proclaim your purity?" He said: I know what you do not know. (2:30)

Everything in creation is one of two pairs. The Qur'an says God has created two of everything and this law applies to all levels of meanings, states and forms. Whatever is discernible and exists is subject to dualities and measures of qualities and quantities. No goodness is free of potential badness and no beginning is without the seeds of its end. The outer world is balanced by an inner world and every form is accompanied by its subtle meaning and purpose.

> And We have created you in pairs. (78:8)

> It is He Who created you from a single self, and from it made its mate, so that he might dwell with her (in love). When they are united, she bears a light load and carries it around. Then when it becomes heavy, they call on Allah their Lord, (saying): "If you grant us a good, (righteous) child, we will be among the

thankful". (7:189)

Our genes, minds and acts may be selfish but our hearts and souls transmit generosity and love. The restless self will only be content when it yields to its soul – ever at peace.

2.3 Levels of Consciousness

You shall certainly travel from stage to stage (84:19)

Every animated creature in our world has a soul and consciousness that determines its position in life. Survival, procreation and growth are amongst the most basic prevalent drives. Creatures have a limited and conditioned consciousness suitable for their role and integration within the universe. Every living entity is driven towards the highest level of consciousness possible to it. Domestic animals draw close to their owners to achieve a higher state of awareness and security. Self-awareness and reflection is a higher level of consciousness. It is evident to a modest degree in primates but in the main it is the preserve of human beings.

It is He Who has made you (His) agents, inheritors of the earth, and raised some of you above others in rank so He can test you regarding what He has given you. Your Lord is swift in retribution and He is Ever Forgiving, Most Merciful. (6:165)

Look how we favour some of them over others (in this world), and for the Hereafter there will be greater degrees and preference. (17:21)

Human beings are unique in being able to relate and connect personal and higher consciousness and thus, reconcile issues appearing contradictory or paradoxical. For example, we may desire immortality, whilst we know that death is inevitable any moment. We look for joy and harmony in a world of conflicts and constant uncertainty and change. Human desire for power and wealth beyond limitations can only be explained by the soul's exposure to boundless power and wealth (God's). Countless perplexing examples can be resolved through the self-soul interplay and the two spheres of consciousnesses – the basic conditioned and the higher consciousness. Why do we like to be depended upon? Why do we like to be independent? Why do we like to be needed? Why do we need others? The self is restless for the soul and desires its blissful peace and constancy. We are composed of lower and higher self and the purpose and challenge of human life is to experience and witness unity and oneness at all times.

> Oh completed (evolved) self, return to your Lord, well-pleased (with him), well-pleasing [Him]. (89:28)

2.4 Death and Higher Consciousness

In ancient times, shamans, seers, rishis, prophets and others endowed with psychic abilities helped to show connections between different levels of consciousness and the subtler states. Dreams, out-of-body and near-death experiences, trance and other unusual states all show the existence of numerous levels of consciousness. Most religions and spiritual paths consider the world, and all that is experienced in it, as a prelude and preparation for another situation that is different and more constant or permanent. Our own world provides us with samples of what there is after death. The more we reflect upon meanings during our life, the smoother and easier our earthly journey will be. In Islam, reflection, prayer, presence of mind and heart and remembrance of God's countless mercies are fundamental to the religion. The Qur'an terms life after death as real or permanent life and the path is based on faith and good work.

The life of this world is nothing but a game and diversion. The abode of the Hereafter, that is truly the life, if only they knew. (29:64)

The Prophet Muhammad taught, 'Prepare for death as it approaches you.' He also said, 'Prepare yourself for the matter you do not know when it will happen,' and, 'Death will reach you, so do not be oblivious.' He also said, 'Send over your riches as charity and you will find it comforting you in the hereafter.' He also advised a man: 'turn away from worldly distractions and be ready for departure from this world'. He also said giving away whatever one loves and to prepare a will also reduces fear of death, and 'Be generous to your relatives and docile and obedient to parents: death will become easy for you and you will never face poverty.' Poverty and needs are both in the inner as well as the outer. An impoverished heart can be more painful than material poverty.

"We have been your friends in the life of this world and are (so) in the Hereafter. Therein you shall have (all) that your inner-selves desire, and therein you shall have (all) for which you ask for. (41:31)

It is Allah Who takes away the souls at the time of their death, and those that die not during their sleep. He keeps those (souls) for which He has ordained death and sends the rest for a term appointed. Verily, in this are signs for a people who think deeply. (39:42)

The Prophet said: 'The best piety in this world is remembrance of death and the best worship is contemplation; the one whose heart overflows with remembering God will find his grave as a part of paradise.' Muslim scholars have consistently urged remembrance of death, as it brings about greater awareness of the present moment and helps with repentance, peace at heart and transformative worship. The Prophet described those who most frequently remember death, and prepare themselves for it, as most intelligent and worthy of honour in this world and the world to come. 'Presence' is the outcome of least self-concern, awareness of the sacredness of the moment and the Reality that is the source of all creation.

But to Allah belongs the last (Hereafter) and the first (this world) (53:25)

The world and its charms are like a mirage or mist veiling Reality. Love of the physical world and material prosperity is like a curtain drawn before our eyes, covering what is beyond it. At the time of death, a person is faced with higher reality and one's own fate, possibly wishing to be given another chance and a new opportunity to wake up to the truth.

Did we not raise high your remembrance? (94:4)

The Prophet taught that we have been created for eternal happiness. He also said that this world is the focus for a blind person who cannot see beyond it. Those who have inner vision are safe from the love of this world, whereas the short-sighted ones gaze continuously upon it. The visionary person takes from it his provision and the foolish person is absorbed in its distractions. After death, nothing will matter except past good deeds and the extent of purity of heart and inner awakening.

But as for anyone who desires the hereafter and strives for it with a striving that it deserves, and he is a believer, the striving of such people will surely be accepted. (17:19)

Death in the prophetic cosmology is the starting point of eternal life. In the next realm, higher consciousness and insights are the equivalent of worldly eyes and other senses. In that world, outer physicality seems a shadow for the inner states which is most clear. On earth, conditioned consciousness and instincts dominate our lives. After death, it is the soul and its higher consciousness and lights that lead us on to the original source – God. Death is a pleasure for true believers because it has moved them from a place of afflictions and uncertainties to a palace of eternal blessings.

Say: "Travel about the earth and see how He started creation. Then later Allah will bring about the next existence (resurrection). Allah is able to do all things." (29:20)

BIRTH AND DEATH

With the birth of a baby, the mind and the ego begin to develop and evolve. With maturity, personal behaviour is refined and is subjected to the mastery of the soul. One of the mechanisms by which this happens is the innate need to balance the outer world with one's own inner state in order to achieve harmony and wellbeingness. This chapter highlights the need for constant reference to the light of the soul within and adherence to transformative faith and uplifting religion. When death of the physical body takes place, the soul with its ego shadow companion, or conditioned consciousness, continues its journey in the hereafter. With death of the body and loss of personal consciousness, all thought or actions are stripped of all the past earthly possibilities. Only past good deeds and the extent of one's spiritual evolvement and readiness are beneficial for the spiritual shift.

> It is God who has created you, and then has provided you with sustenance, and then will cause you to die, and then will bring you to life again. Can any of those beings or powers to whom you ascribe a share in His divinity do any of these things? Limitless is He in His glory, and sublimely exalted above anything to which men may ascribe a share in His divinity! (30:40)

3.1 The One and The Many

From the One source, or singularity, emerged the field of space and time and the dispersion of countless entities and energies. Anything that can be discerned, defined or described reflects conditioned or localized consciousness, drawing its life force from supreme consciousness. Good and bad emanate from unity, split up in space and time to multiplicity and return to unity by merging back to its original singularity.

Whatever exists in creation reflects an aspect of the source from which it has emanated. Whatever begins within time and space will end within time and space, completing the process of exchange between energy and matter, seen and unseen. Indeed, the realm of space-time is the womb which gives birth to every manifestation of the mineral, vegetative, animal and human world. Within this melting pot, everything is conceived, evolves, grows, procreates and then merges back into its original essence.

O you who believe! Do not be like those who disbelieve; for Allah will cause you to regret such a wrong way of life. Allah grants life and causes death, and Allah sees what you do. (3:156)

3.2 Cycles of Birth and Death

The universe is held within space and time which sustains life and creation on earth as we know it. We experience numerous cycles of beginnings and ends, representing different versions of births and deaths. The death of yesterday heralds the birth of today. The underlying essence of all of these motions and commotions is a changeless essence, perfectly constant in harmony, beauty and self-sustaining wholeness. Death naturally follows the original burst of light which produced life. The human soul carries a sacred light that does not end with the death of the body. The physical human body is from the earth and returns to it and the mysterious soul moves on to beyond the confines of space and time.

He brings out the living from the dead, and brings out the dead from the living. And He revives the earth after its death. And thus you shall be brought out (resurrected) (30:19)

From its inception, the human foetus grows and evolves along several stages towards old age and death. The newborn baby soon develops self- consciousness, memory, relationships and its own personality. The body is stimulated and challenged by attraction and repulsion according to what it considers desirable or not by its senses, perception and memory. Peace and contentment implies harmony between the outer world with the inner needs, feelings, intellect and other aspects of the human psyche. Death is like a subtle upward drift in consciousness with an autopilot whose instructions are beyond personal controls. The fuel is what one has gathered in this life in terms of selfless deeds, higher knowledge and extent of enlightenment. Death is a transition from ordinary earthly living to an upgraded life; from limitations to the boundless.

It is He Who gives life, and causes death, and to Him you (all) shall return. (10:56)

Altruism and selfless good deeds are the gateway to transcend the ego and liberation of the self towards its union with the soul; from restriction of a limited and changing identity to the original reality.

We bring the dead to life, and we record what they send ahead and what they leave behind. We have listed everything in a clear register. (36:12)

3.3 Unifying Dualities

The human soul is the gateway that links us to the cosmic soul and access to it is through a purified heart. The self is alive due to the soul which is a sacred spark. Self-soul union helps to explain and reconcile the numerous contradictions, paradoxes and confusions.

Ultimately, the human challenge is based on the need to maintain the balance and stability between outer health and the inner state of the purified heart and the soul within. The healthy human being relates to the outer world as rationally and efficiently as possible, with constant referencing to the inner soul (conscience!). The heart is the connector between soul and self and therefore needs to be maintained pure and clear of tarnish due to negative emotions or attachments. The real challenge is to relate all dualities and see their connections and intrinsic unity.

The blind and the seeing are not the same, nor are those who believe and do good the same as the evil-doers. What little heed they pay! (40:58)

Short-term desires and needs follow a hierarchy ranging from what is material or gross, to subtle and intangible. The priority is to survive and to be healthy, followed by the need to have a clear mind and a pure heart. Ultimately, the final need or desire is to have such inner contentment and joy. This state of bliss is the actual condition of the human soul towards which the self struggles and with surrender (Islam) and unison, the self attains certainty and contentment. Then the challenges of every day life cease to have their previously stressful or depressing impact. This new state in consciousness leads to the joy of witnessing the perfection in every situation and event. Even in pain, the awakened person sees perfection. With this higher perception, the light of unity illumines all shadows of dualities and uncertainties. Human fear of death and desire to know the hereafter relates to the quest for the source and purpose of life. All fears vanish when the self/ego surrenders to the soul.

3.4 Paradoxes of Life

One of the numerous paradoxes in human experience is the love of the old and the new. The timeless and that which is within time are never separate. The absolute and the relative always resonate together. With reflection, we realise that we are attracted to the old and ancient (desire for antique objects and search for personal ancestry and origin) and at the same time desiring the fresh and the new (the air we breathe or the new clothes we like to don). We are trying to bring to proximity the qualities of the soul, which is not subject to time and space, while the desires of self and ego are changeable and thereby look for the new.

And whoever is blind in this world (i.e., does not see Allah's Signs), will be blind in the Hereafter, and more astray from the Path. (17:72)

Every human being is endowed with the innate notion of hope ('tomorrow may be better than today') and reasonable expectations for a better quality of life. However, at the basic level of consciousness and biological evolution, the crude struggle for survival and growth preoccupies the living. It is only with the advent of higher consciousness that morality, ethics and the subtler notions of eternal joy or happiness take shape. This is the domain of higher (God) consciousness.

The most challenging question that faces every human being is to know what dies and what lives on. We can understand that the soul, essence or the original life force may carry on after the death of the body. What dies and perishes is what has been borrowed from earth for a while in order to realise that which is heavenly on earth – the soul and its connection to God – the cosmic soul. Every death is therefore a natural process towards higher consciousness. However, it is the identification with our body and mind over time that makes us fearful of death and imagining it as painful. The child looks for and grasps what it desires; the mature and wise person discovers the Reality (God) that grasps and possesses him. This state is the outcome of faithful surrender! Provisions for the heavenly journey are our selfless deeds on earth.

Say: "Death from which you are fleeing, will certainly catch up with you. Then you will be returned to the Knower of the

Unseen and the Visible and He will inform you about what you did". (62:8)

3.5 Remembering Death

Regular remembrance of death through visits to graveyards or recollections of dead relatives or friends will help to lessen the identification with the physical body and reflect more upon the higher self and the soul. The after-death experience relates to our inner state and its wholesomeness before death. To learn the way of heavens is to serve on earth and aim for sustainable common good. This is how one is saved from the lower self.

We have decreed death for you and We will not be overcome, (56:60)

Or like a rainstorm from the sky, full of darkness, thunder, and lightning. They put their fingers in their ears to keep out the stunning thunderclap, fearful of death... (2:19)

The lightning almost takes away their sight; whenever it shines on them they walk in it, and when it becomes dark to them they stand still; ... Allah has power over all things. (2:20)

The Prophet has described: 'Death for a believer is the best fragrance he has ever smelled, which removes his tiredness and pain completely; and for the unbeliever, it is more painful than a snakebite.' Someone once commented to the Prophet: 'A few people claim that death is more painful than being cut by a saw or crushed by stones.' The Prophet replied, 'It is like that for transgressors.' He also said, 'The easiest death is like un-knotting a loose wool knot.' Furthermore: 'Had the beast been aware (as humans are) of their death, the sons of Adam would not have been allowed to eat their flesh.'

The Prophet advised: "Visit the dying and recite *lâ ilâha illa-'llâh* (there is no god except God). Give them good news of paradise because a good number of people are stunned at their deathbed. At that time, facing the angel of death is harder than having thousands of sword wounds and the soul of a person does not depart from the body until his every vein tastes death.

Imam Ali once preached: 'People, the mercy of Allah be upon you, equip yourself because the departure from this world has been already announced. Why should you be busy with this world after the announcement of departure? Carry your possession and go on board with the best of luggage, which is piety. Fear of death is due to ignorance of its nature. Be sure that death is like washing in a spring: it is like a last chance to rid yourself of your sins and purify yourself of wrong deeds. If death embraces you right now, certainly you will be freed from all sorrow and pain and may attain everlasting happiness and joy.'

> He brings forth the living from the dead and brings forth the dead from the living, and gives life to the earth after its death; in the same way you shall be brought forth. (30:19)

Thus, whilst we are well and alive, we need to regard death as a natural event and go past the habitual denials, fears, anger or depression. We need to practice acceptance and reconciliation with all aspects of life and trust that this inevitable and unknown experience will be pleasant and easy.

> Look then at the signs of Allah's mercy, how He gives life to the earth after its death, truly He will raise the dead to life; and He has power over all things. (30:50)

Death is not a journey to a fearful and dreadful unknown realm but a departure from the struggles and delusions of what we assumed to be real and known. We move from the uncertain, foggy and hazy views of this world to the unifying and clear

state of the next abode. There is no hypocrisy, blame or self-justification there, only a pure soul that experiences this new state
through its lens of a worldly self or personality which it carries as
its legacy of worldly contamination.

Before you come to know who you really are, you need to leave
behind who you are not – a restless self. Then you know you are
soul, which is the source behind all earthly illusions. Death is a
biological fact accompanied by a psychological fear. Sorrow which
is shared becomes lessened. Sharing grief with others bestows a
measure of normality to an unusual event. The presence of close
friends and relatives reinforces the memory of the deceased and
enhances presence of spirit. Thus, this event can be acceptance of a
break with the past as well as remembrance of the inevitable future.

> And He is the Irresistible Supreme, (watching) from above over
> His worshippers, and He sends angels to watch over you; then
> when death comes to one of you, Our Messengers (angel of
> death and his assistants) cause him to die, and they never
> neglect their duty. (6:61)

The term 'life after death' is illogical or contradictory, for life itself
is not subject to death, only birth is. In order to accept that there
is some consciousness or experience after death, we need to give
up the assumption that the exact same person will live again. The
dead person has no doubt undergone major transformation in
form, meaning and consciousness. It is now a soul with traces of
the dead person's mind – a new metamorphosis. In this life we
are like a caterpillar; after death we become a beautiful butterfly,
a clumsy moth or a strange hybrid in between. Apprehension and
concern about death can be a driving force towards greater self-
awareness and accountability or entrapment in fears of the
unknown. In addition, the notions of hell, purgatory and heaven
may influence many of us towards better behaviour and conduct
in this world.

The Qur'an declares:

He Who created death and life that He may test which of you is best in action; He is the All-Mighty, the Ever-Forgiving, (67:2)

Death will always remain a most challenging issue for all of us as no-one has clearly ever come back to give us a comprehensible story. Death is a mirror image of birth in terms of evolvement and reintegration of consciousness. After birth, the mind begins developing consciousness, giving rise to a full-blown ego with its particular preferences and views. At death this personal conditioned consciousness or ego sinks into and merges with its soul consciousness, which then drifts towards its divine origin of unity.

Are they not guided by the many generations that We have destroyed before them, among whose dwelling places they walk about? There are signs in that for people of sound intellect. (20:128)

And the ultimate end is with your Lord. (53:42)

3.6 Death as Freedom

The original absolute singularity, which is non-spatial and non-temporal is also present now, except that it is veiled by countless pluralities.

We have [indeed] decreed that death shall be [ever-present] among you: and there is nothing to prevent Us (56:60)

Death is often described as relief or liberation but who is being liberated and by what means? If it is from suffering and pain one needs to ask: who is it that suffers and what is the real cause? The human body is balanced between health and illness. There are more bacteria and germs in us than the trillion cells of the body. Death is the gateway to convergence and unity after the period of challenges and exposures to earthly uncertainties. It is therefore a closure to confusion and an opening to fusion: an end to ignorance and conflicting shadows and a window onto the vistas of lights, primary patterns and foundations and the essence of existence. Death strips off the muddles, cover-ups, denials, other props and egotistic trappings that bestows individual false identities. At the outset of death, an unusual clarity and vibrancy sets in. The Qur'an describes death as the real awakening, while the Prophet instructs: 'Die before you die'. Wake up to the permanent and die to the temporal.

Everyone shall taste death. Then to Us you shall be returned. (29:57)

In our present time and culture, death is often hidden and camouflaged to lessen the importance of the need to remember it and prepare for it ahead of time. In the West, the general habit is that of denial. To remember death is bad for consumerism. Contemporary life has medicated and institutionalised the process of birth as well as that of dying. Thus, we have separated birth from death and have isolated these major events from everyday life at home and in the community. Traditional habits and religious practices have also been modified and changed to accommodate personal preferences and egotistic desires. The increase in the practice of cremation and legalised euthanasia are examples of new trends. Islam only allows normal burial after washing the dead body, clothing it with a shroud and praying upon it. Respect for the dead body is a reflection of respect for the sacred soul that was living in it whilst alive.

Say: "My prayer and my sacrifice (acts of worship), my life and my death, are all for Allah, the Lord of the worlds; (6:162)

HUMAN NATURE

We have shown him (human beings) the Way: (he is) either grateful or ungrateful. (76:3)

We have guided his Way

In this chapter, we reflect upon the nature of man – composed of a soul and its reflection, the self. The soul and its light of pure consciousness energises its evolving self as conditioned consciousness, which in turn gives life to the body and the mind and the changing personality. As the body and the ego develop and mature, the natural progression is for the self to seek attributes possessed by the soul. Eventually, the self may learn to submit to the soul and thereby rest contentedly with the divine attributes. By surrendering to the soul, these attributes appear within the self as higher qualities or traits – part of higher consciousness. The human potential is then fulfilled – earthly of heavenly origin.

4.1 Body, Mind and Soul

Have they not travelled in the land so that their hearts (and intellect) may thus learn wisdom, and their ears may thus learn to hear (Truth)? It is not eyes that are blind, but hearts in their breasts which are blind. (22:46)

Every human being has a visible, tangible and physical outer form, as well as a mind, an inner heart and a soul. The body, its structures and the brain, which is the physical base of the mind and intellect, are all dependent upon a subtler 'inner' heart which is the abode of the soul. These different aspects of the human makeup are in perpetual dynamic interaction. The Qur'an describes human inception, makeup, purpose and evolvement as:

Successful indeed are the believers, those who humble themselves in their prayer, and who turn away from all that is frivolous, and who are intent on inner purity; and who are mindful of their chastity, [not giving way to their desires] with anyone but their spouses - that is, those whom they rightfully possess [through wedlock]: in which case they are free of all blame, whereas those who seek to go beyond that [limit] are truly transgressors; those who honour their trusts and their contracts, and who guard their prayers [from all worldly intent]. It is these people, who will inherit paradise, remaining there shall timelessly forever. We created man out of the essence of clay, and then made him a drop of sperm in a secure receptacle [the womb], and then formed the drop into a clot, and then formed the clot into a lump, and formed the lump into bones, and clothed the bones in flesh - and then brought him into being as a new creation: Then subsequently, you will certainly die; then, you shall be raised from the dead on Resurrection Day. (23:1-16)

The human soul is linked at one level to the cosmic soul and supreme consciousness and at another level to the self as composed of body and its organs, mind, senses and intellect. The human soul is the source of life and contains all the desirable attributes and qualities, which the self and ego yearn for. Although the nature of the soul is not subject to limitations and fluctuations of time and space, it is entrapped for a while within space-time boundaries. Even though the soul carries the divine imprint of the absolute, its power is only manifest through limited personal conditioned awareness, action and will. It is like a celestial hologram programmed to cause all the functions of the terrestrial entity. The soul is the interlink between the physical human being (with all its worldly limitations) and God's boundlessness, grace and attributes. The soul knows all about the Lord of creation and is in total obedience and linked with Him.

Allah thus makes clear to you His signs that you may understand. (2:242)

It is human nature to strive for survival, growth, power, ongoingness and so on, as well as meaning and purpose of life and the hereafter. The soul acts as God's agent or representative within us. For a human being to act as God's steward on earth implies total accountability to the soul (inner conscience) with a clear head and a pure heart. Such a being must act appropriately and reflectively at all times. This awareness is needed to maintain stewardship, balance and justice in creation. A companion of the Prophet once enquired: 'Who is the most intelligent and honourable person?' He replied: 'Those who most frequently remember death and prepare themselves for it, they will be the most honoured in this world and the world to come.'

.......................and the abode of the hereafter is better for those who guard themselves (against evil). Will you not use your intellect? - As for those who hold fast to the Book and keep up prayer, We will not waste the reward of the right doers. (7:169-170)

The wellbeingness of a person relates to bodily health, mental clarity, emotional stability, rational balance and integrity. The mind functions efficiently when it recalls appropriate memory and relates it to outer events as perceived and evaluated. At all times, the human being is challenged to balance the inner state with outer worldly conditions, using the soul at all times as a reference and for inner calibration. Thus, the more frequent is the connection between the self and the soul, the more wholesome and balanced is the person. The soul is a sacred light within the human heart, which when it is well, then all is well.'

Who fears the Beneficent Allah in secret and comes with a

penitent heart. (50:33)

4.2 Similarity of Human Souls

The underlying foundation of relationships between human beings is the sameness of all souls. Each person has a unique body, mind and personality, as a result of the interaction of nature and nurture to varying degrees of preponderance. Yet, we can relate to all other human beings due to the intrinsic sameness of our souls or spirit. The less we look for outer differences, the more we realise our inner similarities, such as the pursuit of contentment and happiness. We echo common needs, desires and ideals, yet we are all different in the way we pursue these goals.

> O people! be careful of (your duty to) your Lord, Who created you from one self and from it created its mate and spread from these two, many men and women; and be careful of (your duty to) Allah, in whose name you make demands of one another, and also in respect of your families; Allah Watches over you continually. (4:1)

Early on in childhood, we mostly experience simple sensations. Later on, emotions, memory, preferences and other mental states develop. Our five senses are like rivers that pour their input to a lake that correlates them, giving rise to discernment and evaluations that change with time. This inner sense is called the combining sense. With maturity, whenever a sensation occurs, an instantaneous reference is made to the relevant memory for a more reliable perception and appropriate response.

Wisdom, justice and truth are close together. Absolute truth never changes, but is experienced as relative. Justice is to do the right thing, in the right way and at the right time. Wisdom is both worldly as well as heavenly. A person may have a great deal of worldly experience and wisdom, whereas spiritual insight or higher wisdom implies vision and access to truth. Worldly efficiencies are according to context, whereas heavenly insights transcend all circumstances. Reference to the human soul or divine attributes brings about that higher realization.

> Say: "Mankind! Now truth (i.e. the Qur'an and Prophet Muhammad SAW), has come to you from your Lord. Whoever is guided, is only guided for his own good, and whoever goes astray, he does so to his own loss, and I am not (set) as a custodian over you." (10:108)

4.3 The Changing and The Constant

The most desired human condition is comfort and ease. This is the permanent condition of our soul within. The self is in constant struggle to attain that state. All worldly experiences and realities are relative and subject to change. Every aspect of our perception, as such, is relative and changeable. Constancy belongs to higher (soul) consciousness. Whatever we experience or sense is within an energy field that had originally descended from a unifying essence. In our worldly endeavours we differentiate, separate, categorise and classify. In truth, however, whatever appears to be separate or different is in essence connected, albeit at great distance in space or time. The Prophet was asked about the state before creation and he said there was God within 'misty air', where there was no perceptibility or discernibility. Spiritual maturity implies having gained the insight that every duality or separation stems from One essential unity, leads to it and is sustained by it.

> And that those who have been given knowledge will know that it (this Qur'an) is the truth from your Lord, and that they may believe in it, and their hearts may submit to it with humility. Allah is the Guide of those who believe, in the Straight Path. (22:54)

A mature person relies on reason, rationality and context as far as earthly affairs are concerned. Life's experiences bring forth and demonstrate the logic of interplay between cause and effect. Then, there are reasons that go beyond normal comprehension, intellect or logic. Spiritual logic or insight may have little in common with common rationality.

And the Word of your Lord has been fulfilled in truth and in justice. None can change His Words. And He is the All-Hearer, the All-Knower. (6:115)

Suffering implies pain, disturbance, discord, chaos, confusion or breakdown in connectivity. It is like an outer bitter shell that needs to be broken through in order to reach its inner meaning and purpose. Our world is like a melting pot in which every entity aspires to reach its stability and wholesomeness at all levels, from the gross to the most subtle. The ultimate state of consistent inner contentment and peace will be attained when the self or ego totally submits to the soul and, therefore, accesses at all times higher consciousness and perfections. Then only will fears and sorrow cease and the state of ever-present joy is discovered.

Words such as 'belief', 'faith', 'trust' or other religious terms imply a connection with the heart or soul in anticipation of guidance beyond the mind. The outer world appears chaotic because of all the dualities and apparent conflicts in forms and energies. Yet, in truth, there is always perfect order within what appears to be chaotic. To perceive the unifying field of opposites, we need to view situations from a higher level of perception or consciousness. The uncertainty within the inner atom is at the root of relative certainty and predictability of physical, worldly realities. These two domains are ever together in creation. All dualities emanate from unity and return to it.

The world will be seen as harmonious if we look through the

lens of the ever-harmonious soul. Chemistry is the science of entities and matter, whereas physics is the science of energy and force – they complement each other. The essence of their different foundations is based upon light and motion, which relate to space and time, and produce what we experience as the world of forms and meaning. When we relate the outer world to the inner soul, we bypass the usual emotional developments and begin to see creation with greater clarity. The mind is to be used for rational and sensible issues. Otherwise, the ego will produce emotional pain. Worldly pleasures are naturally complemented by displeasure, unless they lead to durable joy and inner bliss beyond the mind. Imam Ali had said: "Let your (higher) self guard over you: your limbs are "watchmen" and truthful scribes and are recording your acts and the number of your breaths. The utter darkness cannot hide you from them nor can closed doors hinder their vision. Surely tomorrow is very close to this day."

… Or can the darkness and the light be equal? … Say: Allah is the Creator of all things, and He is the One, the Supreme. (13:16)

4.4 Soul Guidance
Throughout human history, teachers, sages, prophets, philosophers and community leaders have worked for the common good and to bring about a stable and happy society. Most religions presented programmes or teachings that could be practiced by the public to enhance their wellbeing, contentment and happiness. The model of the self-soul complementing duality preceded the Abrahamic teachings (approximately 4000 years ago) and is often reflected in many ancient cultures and religions with some modification or adjustment.

You will not find people who believe in Allah and the Last Day, making friendship with those who oppose Allah and His Messenger, even though they were their fathers, their sons, their brothers, or their kindred. For such people He has written Faith in their hearts, and strengthened them with spirit from Himself. And He will admit them to Gardens under which rivers flow, to dwell in (forever). Allah is pleased with them, and they with Him. Such people are the Party of Allah. Truly, it is the Party of Allah who will be the successful. (58:22)

Just before he died from drinking the poison hemlock, Socrates sat and talked quietly with some of his friends (including Plato) and cheerfully spoke about life after death and the immortality of the soul. The ancient Greek word for 'alive' is the same as the word 'ensouled'. The earliest philosophical view was that the soul was what made living things sentient or alive. Plato considered the soul to be the essence of a person that reasons, decides and acts. He considered this essence to be an occupant of the body with its own separate, immortal existence. From ancient time, contemplating and inspired human beings had deep intuition and insight regarding the dual nature of man. Later, religious revelations (books) presented a more detailed package of transcendental truth.

We revealed to you an inspired book by our Command. You did not know what the book was nor (what) the faith (was), but we made it a light by which We guide whom we please... (42:52)

Aristotle, following Plato, defined the soul as the core essence of a being but argued against it having a separate existence. For instance, if a knife had a soul, the act of cutting would be that soul, because 'cutting' is the essence of what it is to be a knife. Unlike Plato and religious traditions, he did not consider the soul to be some kind of separate ghostly occupant of the body (just as the act of cutting cannot be separated from the knife). As the soul is an activity of the body, it cannot be immortal (when a knife is destroyed, the cutting stops). To be more exact, the soul is the 'the first activity' of a living body. This is a state or a potential for actual or 'second activity'. 'The axe has an edge for cutting' was, for Aristotle, analogous to 'humans have bodies for rational activity and the potential for rational activity thus constitutes the essence of a human soul'.

> And they ask you about the soul. Say: The soul is from the command of my Lord and you (mankind) have only been given a little knowledge. (17:85)

Many Christian scholars hold, as Aristotle did, that to attain any assured knowledge of the soul is one of the most difficult things in the world. Saint Augustine wrote that the soul is: 'a special substance, endowed with reason, adapted to rule the body'. Medieval Christian thinkers often assigned to the soul attributes such as thought and imagination, as well as faith and love. This suggests that the boundaries between mind and soul can vary in different interpretations. Whatever one experiences, senses or perceives in the outer world has its innate pattern and intrinsic design within the soul. In fact, as we move along space/time in the world, we are retracing the dormant pattern of archetypal possibilities within us.

4.5 Islamic Cosmology of The Self

In Islam, the Qur'an and the Prophetic teachings describe the human being as a composite of light (soul), which is only good and its shadow (self), which can be nasty and decadent or noble through grooming, submission and obedience. The self or ego can only be reformed by discipline, refinement, accountability, awareness, regular worship and 'God orientation'.

The Qur'an explains:

> "My sons! Go and enquire about Joseph and his brother, and never give up hope of Allah's Mercy. No one despairs of Allah's

63

Mercy, except the people who disbelieve." (12:87)

(There is for him) rest and plenty of provision, and a Garden of delights.
 (56:89)

And the self and how it is constructed; inspired to be decadent or faithful. (91:8)

Surely! man was created anxious (restless), (70:19)

Every human being will taste death; We test you through the bad and the good [things of life] by way of trial: and to Us you must return. (21:35)

Numerous other verses in the Qur'an describe the need for the self to be disciplined and taught to know, adore and worship the Creator who has placed within the breast of the human being a soul (breath of the Lord). The Prophetic teachings emphasise the importance of a purified heart and a generous self as a preparation for death and the hereafter. Islamic teaching presents many prescriptions and checklists to purify the heart through awareness, selfless actions and repentance and thereby let the light of the soul bring about higher self-awareness and spiritual insights.

... (He succeeds) who comes to Allah with a wholesome heart. (26:89)

Generosity towards one's friends is easy and commonly practiced. Generosity towards one's enemy requires one to transcend beyond judgment and values to the point of accepting that the enemy also harbours a soul, which is as sacred as one's own. The Qur'an specifically mentions that when one looks upon one's enemy as though he is an intimate friend, one is on the path of enlightenment. Then, he who is separated from you by enmity is regarded as a dear friend.

> A good action and a bad action are not the same. Repel the bad with something better, and if there is enmity between you and someone else, he will be like a warm friend. (41:34)

The heart of the enlightened person overflows with light and insights; this is the universal being that has completed the purpose of life's journey. When the heart has no impurities, such as anger, fear, lust, acquisitiveness and other vices, then actions become expressions of justice and goodness. Appropriate action produces no fears, regrets or other negative considerations, except perfection at that instant. The short-lived instant is but a flash of the sacred constant – the ever-present moment travels in time from timelessness.

> Those who believe and whose hearts find peace by the remembrance of Allah; only in the remembrance of Allah do hearts find peace. (13:28)

> O Prophet! say to those you are holding captive: If Allah knows of any good in your hearts, He will give you something better than what has been taken away from you and will forgive you, and Allah is Forgiving, Merciful. (8:70)

> Know that the Messenger of Allah is among you. If he were to obey you in many things, you would suffer for it, but Allah has given you love of Faith and has made it beautiful in your hearts, and has made disbelief, wickedness and disobedience hateful to you. Such people are the rightly guided ones, (49:7)

THE ETERNAL QUEST

All of us, human beings, are driven to attain long-lasting wellbeing and happiness. This is a challenging process involving life's multifaceted experiences and uncertainties. As the self evolves towards higher consciousness, it begins to submit to the soul (and its Lord). Now, it can be said that there are glimpses of eternal presence. To be present means to face eternity or to be at the threshold of time. The consequence of this is a deep sense of oneness, peace and happiness. This is transformation and enlightenment. To do one's best requires total presence, or absence from everything else, then the doer and what is being done are in unison – an eternal instant.

5.1 Self-Soul Relationships

Outer expressions of joy and happiness simply indicate an aspect of self-soul closeness, peace and inner joy. Every human being seeks durable fulfilment. The soul within every human being is always stable, content and perfect. The Qur'an describes souls as having been exposed to the Lord and have known divine supremacy and God's attributes. Thus, some fulfilment will occur naturally when the self relates to the soul and some tranquillity and peace is experienced. The more the self yields to the soul and resonates with it, the more contentment and happiness is experienced. This desired state of wholesomeness is due to the self's abandonment of its (illusory) separation, independence or outer distractions. Unison between the shadowy self and constant soul is the last step in spiritual completeness.

There! Every self will be tried for what it did before, and they will be returned to Allah, their rightful Lord, and their invented false deities will vanish from them. (10:30)

66

5.2 Aspiring to The Highest

Every sentient entity in the world has an innate drive to be stable and to reach its maximum potential in consciousness. Therefore, if we consider that the foundation and source of all creation is the universal or cosmic soul (from which countless souls have emerged), we can then say that each of these souls reflects a certain aspect or quality of the universal or cosmic soul. Rest and peace will be found when harmonious synchrony with the cosmic soul is attained through the personal soul. This is the meaning of religious people saying that only when you are with God (or God's will) do you have real peace and contentment. The Qur'an declares that 'real rest is only when you are with your Lord'.

Unto your Lord, on that day, will be the final settlement. (75:12)

Life is experienced within the flow of time and, therefore, it is sacred for it overflows from eternity. Space-time is the sublime womb from which the miracle of bliss is born. This is life's purpose. Maturity and wisdom begin with discerning what is good or bad in different contexts, aiming for durable goodness for all concerned. If we consider that the cosmic soul (or God) is eternally in a state of perfection, contentment and joy, then the happiness of every individual human being is according to the ability to be in unison with its soul within, for every soul is a sacred spark from God. The ever-changing human (conditioned) consciousness aspires towards higher consciousness, which is constant, pure and ever-present within the soul. This is the meaning of Divine presence and the sacredness of life. The Qur'an says: 'And wherever you turn is the face of Allah,' and, "He is with you wherever you are."

The Companions of the Garden on that day will be graced with a better abode and a better resting place. (25:24)

Whoever hopes for the Meeting with Allah, then Allah's appointed time is certainly coming. He is the All-Hearer, the All-Knower. (29:5)

Hence, human fulfilment can be measured according to the extent of personal awareness of and subordination to the ever-presence of supreme consciousness. Unison of self and soul comes about as a result of transcending all aspects of duality, causality, and other matters relating to creation and existence. To be recharged spiritually we need first to disconnect with anything (all senses, thoughts or feelings) which causes distraction or change. The self can then naturally yield and unite with its soul mate with ease and trust. Blissful contentment is a result of that union.

Happiness is often experienced as the outcome of helping and serving others with no expectations. The lower self can then transcend to the higher. The mystery of consciousness is beyond our minds to grasp, as it is the source and cause of mind. However, we can gain some idea of its nature when we consider its different levels, spheres, attributes and manifestations. These are countless in quality and extent but all stem from a supreme, universal consciousness. Within all of these fields of consciousnesses, the original absolute consciousness is also ever-present. All limited or conditioned consciousnesses are possible due to absolute or supreme consciousness. The human soul is ever connected with the unfathomable cosmic soul. Yet, we humans try to personalise God and use religion for worldly gains and powers as some priests do!

And remember your Lord within yourself humbly and fearfully and in a voice not loud, in the morning and the afternoon, and do not be one of the unaware. (7:205)

No just estimate of Allah do they make when they say: Allah has not revealed anything to a human being. Say: Who revealed the

Book which Moses brought, as a light and guidance to people, but which you put down on sheets of paper to display, while concealing much?............... (6:91)

5.3 The Constant Reference Point

Authenticity and stability of a human being implies a degree of constancy and reliability due to reference and reflection of the soul's steady state. 'Presence' is due to the spontaneous reference to, and awareness of, that which is eternally present: the supreme consciousness via soul consciousness. The so-called 'I' changes and yet something within the 'I' does not change. Yesterday's 'I' has died and today's 'I' is different and yet, 'I' refers to a point of sameness. This state of paradox is a reflection that Truth (or supreme consciousness) never changes, but what emanates from it—such as the self or ego—changes constantly. Every soul is aware, perpetually, of its eternal nature and transmits that energy wave to every cell in mind and body. The challenge of individual human life is to align body, mind and personal consciousness to its essence and root cause – pure consciousness.

Both east and west belong to Allah, so wherever you turn there is the face of Allah. Surely! Allah is All-Sufficient for His creatures' needs, All-Knowing. (2:115)

To be in constant gratitude and patience is to be at the edge of witnessing perfection – the essence of the soul. Through the lens of the soul only perfection is seen. The idea of reference to soul or God simply means calibrating one's personal consciousness with the pure or supreme consciousness. Most spiritual and religious practices entail accessing higher consciousness by turning away from the conditioned and relative. Informal or ritualistic prayers imply leaving behind worldly consciousness and journeying towards pure consciousness. This is how we can place our worldly affairs in proper perspective. The human mind is designed to deal with dualities and to grapple with cause and effect and other causal manifestations. For a child, the loss of a sweet seems important but not so for a grown-up, because of difference in perspective. Thus, when we compare our worldly affairs, which are relative, to the higher zone close to the absolute, then a fresh attitude will set in; the urgency or the extent of stress regarding many matters will simply vanish. In religion it is often mentioned that we need to refer important matters to God, implying precisely this exercise. All belongs to God, emanates and returns to Him.

He Who created the seven heavens in layers. You will not find any flaw in the creation of the Most Beneficent. Then look again: Can you see any rifts? (67:3)

5.4 Resolving the Paradox

Light and other forms of energy and matter are caught within the confines of time and space. The mystery of life and creation can be traced at the boundaries of space and time and in the original and ever-present sacred void. The human tendency of wanting to stretch a good time eternally or to stop a 'bad' time instantly echoes the quest to break out of space-time limitations. It is natural for conditioned consciousness to lead to what is past worldly limitations to the zone of transcendental pure consciousness. The healthy seeker connects all aspects of relative sensation to the timeless state of inner perception, the soul's insight or Divine light.

He grants wisdom to whom He pleases, and whoever is granted wisdom, he indeed is given abundant goodness …………. (2:269)

Another paradox in human experience is that of the old and the new. The timeless and that which is within time are never separate since the absolute and the relative always resonate together. We seek the most old and ancient, as well as that which is 'now', fresh and new. Both of these time-related ideas disappear when we catch a glimpse of the eternally perfect instant. This is why it is said that there is no merit in abstentions, unless they lead to spiritual awakening. The death of the ego is the birth of the enlightened self – a new life.

5.5 The Ever-Present

God is One, meaning the supreme consciousness is unified, eternal, absolute and unique. The human soul reflects this true unique oneness. Real presence implies that which is pervasive everywhere and at all times; thus, presence implies the ever-present sacred essence or Divine presence. There is no 'otherness' in that field or state. The Qur'an says: 'He is closer to you than your jugular vein.' Islam is founded upon the declaration that there is no true Reality except that of God. Every created entity is as alive, aware and present to the extent of its submission (Islam) and abandonment or surrender into this sacred light. Remembrance of this truth is echoed in every aspect of life, belief and worship. When we realise that the source of all mercy and grace is Allah, then *barakah* (extra grace) flows and bestows spiritual glow upon the event.

It is He Who created the heavens and the earth in six days (periods) and then established Himself over the Throne (with complete control and command). He knows what goes into the earth and what comes out of it, what descends from the heaven and what goes up to it. And He is with you wherever you are. And Allah Sees what you do. (57:4)

5.6 The Next Life

The Qur'an declares our short earthly life as a prelude to an everlasting or durable state after death. Islamic worship and practices enhance the heart's purity and presence and, thereby, promote clarity in intention and direction at all times. This state of heightened awareness and self-reflection brings about the qualities of selflessness, generosity, courage and love of truth. Love unifies and connects all diverse entities. Allah created the universe out of love for His amazing attributes to be known and adored. He is the source of all that unifies the universe.

Allah will bring forth people whom He loves and they love Him. (5:54)

Islam is based upon love and respect for the Qur'an, its regular study, recitation and living according to its teachings. It is the duty of parents to encourage their children to learn and apply the Qur'anic knowledge, signs and insights to their everyday life. To hear, accept and follow the message with faith and trust will bring about transformation and a renewed state and life. The Qur'an is a revealed book of signs that transmits at several levels, from the obvious to the most sublime.

Yes, the friends of Allah will feel no fear and neither shall they grieve: (10:62)

The Prophet Muhammad has mentioned that people do not like death because, they are not ready to meet God, the Almighty. He also said: 'There are two types of people: When a believer dies, he is relieved from the agony of this world; and when a disbeliever dies, trees, beasts and other creatures feel ease.' Similarly, Imam Ali said: 'The death of a pious person is a source of comfort for him, while the death of an impious person is a comfort for other people'.

The Prophet also said: 'That person will be most close to me on the Day of Judgment who is most truthful, most prompt in returning the entrusted things, who keeps his promise, who is the best in manners, and who has good relationships with other people.'; and: 'No deed is better regarded than good behaviour when placed in the balance on the Day of Judgment.'; and lastly: 'The most truthful, the most trustworthy, those with the best behaviour, and good relations with other people, are close to me.'

Those who give (in alms), what they are given, with their hearts fearful, because they will return to their Lord. (23:60)

Refinement of character and good behaviour are considered as the foundation of living the religion of Islam. This is how outer information regarding the religious teachings and laws can lead to inner transformation and enlightenment.

Sacredness of Life

Because of this We decreed for the children of Israel that if anyone kills another person – unless it is in punishment for murder or for spreading corruption on earth – it is as if he had killed all mankind; whereas, if anyone saves a life, it will be as if he had saved all of mankind. (5:32)

A person may desire death due to poor health (mental or physical) or unfavourable circumstances such as hardship, suffering and other causes of anguish and misery. Islam discourages such a wish and any act that may lead to deliberate death. According to Islamic teachings, it is the duty of the close relatives to take care of such a person and help to comfort or restore him. If the relatives are unable to do this, then it is the duty of the community to help.

The Prophet Muhammad said: 'No one should wish for death due to the misfortune he is facing; if necessary he may say: "God keep me alive as long as it is better for me, and afflict me with death whenever it is good for me".' He also said, 'Do not wish for death. If you are a good person, then it is better for you to add more to your good deeds. But if you are not a good person, then it is better for you if punishment is delayed, therefore do not desire death.' Patience (an aspect of timelessness) is one of Allah's names.

O you who have faith! What is the matter with you that, when you are told: "Go out and fight (struggle) in the name of Allah," you cling heavily to the earth? Are you happier with this world than with the life to come? Yet the enjoyment of life in this world is but a small thing when compared with the life to come! (9:38)

Every human being is endowed with the innate notion of hope and reasonable expectations of life. At the level of biological evolution, the crude struggle for survival and growth preoccupies the living entity. It is only with the advent of higher consciousness (Adam) that the notions of joy and happiness take place. Our life on earth will be purposeful if we aim to attain this state with both head and heart. This world is but a practice for the hereafter.

"O my people! This worldly life is a fleeting enjoyment, whereas the life to come is the abode of permanence. (40:39)

TWILIGHT AND DEATH

Death is a certainty for every entity that is born. Nevertheless, most of us remain afraid of death. The numerous reasons for this fear start with attachments to the familiar world of body and mind and what is around us. The uncertainty and natural ignorance about the event of death is another common reason – we fear what we don't know, hence we are most apprehensive about what happens after death. For the spiritually evolved person, death can be seen as signifying a new birth to where time and space are suspended. The experience of inner feelings, the outer world and wilful action are suspended with death.

The condition of the self in this new state depends on the level of its evolvement in consciousness. The greater is one's spiritual progress on earth, the easier the crossing into the heavens. Our intentions, actions and thoughts are the provisions for the journey to the hereafter. Good and virtuous actions, transcending the lower self serve as the currency for the passage to the next realm, which leads to the source of oneness. As we don't know what lies at the end of the tunnel of death, we are in fear of it. What is at the entrance of the tunnel is also at its exit – truth has no beginning or end.

And the stupor of death brings with it the truth (the state) which you were trying to avoid. (50:19)

6.1 Overcoming Fear of Death

We fear what we don't know and we are sorry for not acting with grace and experiencing perfection. The desire to prolong life on earth is due to being trapped within lower consciousness. To overcome worldly illusions without a clear path towards liberation, one needs to transcend the limitations of space and time. As death is the inevitable conclusion to birth, it is only logical that we should prepare for it, especially in old age. However, most of us avoid remembrance of death due to fears and uncertainties of the lower self. Unless we experience openings of higher consciousness through prayers, meditation and acts that diminish ego awareness, we remain apprehensive about death. The majority of us express sorrow for a person's death, even though it was timely and brought relief to the deceased. It is, of course, the ones still living who are pained due to the departure of a loved one. Also, the feelings and emotions of a dying person may include rejection or denial of what is happening ("why me?!") as well as anger, depression and despondency. Those who are ready and cheerful about departure are described in the Qur'an:

> The great fearful event (Day of Resurrection) will not grieve them and the angels will receive them with The Greeting. "This is your Day [of triumph] which you were promised!" (21:103)

To succeed in what is unknown, one must first understand and abide by what is known. To be free inwardly, one must accept limitations and responsibility outwardly. If one denies form or meanings, one is denied essence and death is the one way, or the door, that leads to the essence. Most of us are concerned about preserving life as we are familiar with, and attached to, its manifestations. We like to repeat what we have enjoyed in the past and carry memories and desires which bestow a feeling of continuity to our present day life. Personal preferences, familiarities and identity are natural developments, which can later become barriers to higher consciousness and healthy acceptance of death.

> When we heard the Guidance (this Qur'an), we believed in it, and who ever believes in his Lord will have no fear, either of a decrease in the reward of his good deeds or an increase in punishment for his sins. (72:13)

With maturity and wisdom, the relationship with one's body, or strong identity with it, becomes less important. Attention to one's inner state and the relationship with heart and soul and subtler realities gain priority with age. The more a wise person cultivates the higher self and purifies the heart, thereby accessing the soul and its light, the easier it will be to submit to death. Such a practice will reveal the soul's boundlessness and sacredness and the body's transience. It can even make death a welcome event.

> Men who are not distracted by trade or sales from the Remembrance of Allah, nor from performing prayers, nor from giving the Zakat. They fear a Day when hearts and eyes will be in turmoil. (24:37)

During our lifetime, we are given many glimpses and hints of ongoingness and life after death. The concept of foreverness or eternity appears often in our life's dealings. We are naturally drawn to 'eternal love', longevity or immortality. The process of displacing attachment to this world with insights into the after world is no doubt of great help in preparing for death and befriending it. The wise person is well prepared at all levels of relationships (to self or family) to leave this world when the time comes. Insights to the unseen and the intangible realms naturally reduce fears and apprehensions of death. A reflective person can realise that this life is but a sample and prelude to the hereafter. The terror of mortality begins to vanish as the light of the soul shines upon all dualities and reveals the essential unity and oneness in creation. The Qur'an describes such a person:

> Surely, I did know that [one day] I would have to face my account! (69:20)

> .... so surely there will come to you a guidance from Me,

then whoever follows My guidance, no fear will come upon them, nor will they grieve. (2:38)

6.2 Courtesies Towards the Dying

As for the duties of people around the person who is dying, proper intention and courtesy are most important. Sincerity, steady emotions and concern for the peace and ease of departure are essential. It is important to have an atmosphere of pleasantness and tranquillity in the place where the departing person is resting. The newborn child is received with joy and good anticipation. By celebrating quietly the departure of the dying person, we will have participated appropriately in completing the repetitive worldly story. All is well that ends well. In truth, there is only Divine perfection and grace at all times everywhere. Whatever exists reflects an aspect of eternal perfection and moves towards final perfection. In recent literature, many guidelines and useful advice are given to the friends and family of the dying person. When in the presence of a dying person, try to place yourself in their position. Are you at ease, relaxed, confidently subdued and in submission?

6.3 What Happens After Death?

Birth is the emergence of a living entity from the secure aqueous enclosure of the womb into a world of changes, uncertainties and the need to survive and grow. The emergence from the womb to the world outside is repeated in reverse when we die and leave the body behind to emerge into the field of eternal consciousness. Thus, one can say there are two births; one from the mother's womb and the other from the human material form. Islam also proposes two deaths: the physical and personal in this world and the other is collective and universal just before resurrection.

In this world, we are accustomed to choice, action, acquisitions, new knowledge and experience as a result of natural interactions. After death, all such possibilities cease. We no longer encounter any dualities or worldly causalities. What we experience is a new state, without the worldly boundaries of time and space. The Qur'an describes this realm as a new creation leading to eternity. The state of the deceased person in the grave is considered as a continuation and completion of the state before death. The Prophet has warned that a person's condition in the grave follows from one's state in life. If a person was content and reconciled in life, then this same disposition will carry on after death. Naturally, the last hours, days and weeks are what matter most. The Prophet has highlighted the importance of the latter period in one's life. He has said that if you repent and wake up to the Truth, even a moment before death, you are saved. The dying person will have some idea before death about the forthcoming state after death.

Death means the separation of soul from body and all material connections, which were facilitated through self and soul. The overall state of the mind, and what we call personality, will move on in a modified way with the soul, like a veil. The soul itself remains ever pure and eternal but is now carrying with it the traces of the conditioned consciousness of the dead person. The soul is like a light and its worldly experiences and conditioning like a sheath upon it. According to the transparency (purity) of this veil will be the ease of the soul's journey. The best preparation is through the heart's purity and its freedom from attachments, desires, expectations, fears and worldly concerns.

In this life, we are conditioned by our mind, body and habits and thus, we act according to certain measures of reason, logic and rationality. After death, we are stripped of all our senses and powers like a passive observer whose state or condition is already determined beforehand.

In most religious and spiritual paths, much emphasis is placed upon readiness for the next world. Most of these teachings confirm the importance of access to soul or God consciousness whilst on earth. When the senses and other faculties begin to shut down then insight—the light of the soul—becomes the guide to the new experience. Acts of meditation, prayer, worship, deep reflection, out-of-body experiences, near-death experiences and many other religious acts of devotion are all helpful in preparing for this inevitable major transition. Personal spiritual enlightenment in this world is ultimately the best preparation for the metamorphosis into the new life. It is said that the night for the ignorant is like the day for the enlightened and the day of the ignorant is a night for the enlightened. One is a prisoner in this world, and the other is liberated from it. One is caught by senses and sight and the other by light of insight.

> Those who believe (in Islam), as well as those who follow the Jewish faith, and the Christians, and the Sabeans, whoever believing in God and the last day and does good, they will have their reward from their Lord, and there is no fear for them, nor will they grieve. (2:62)

6.4 Near-Death Experiences

There have been numerous attempts to investigate any direct evidence regarding the soul's journey to life after death. There is, however, no scientific or rational proof, even when we consider the countless reports of near death experiences (NDEs) and the noticeable impact of such experiences upon the recipients. However, the lack of tangible evidence of the soul's journey to the hereafter does not nullify this plausible possibility. The majority of mankind look for evidence to increase their faith in the hereafter and eternal life. We like to 'believe' and have faith – it is comforting.

> And on the earth are signs for those who have Faith with certainty – And also in your own selves. Will you not then see? (51:20-21)

The idea of life after death, as experienced or imagined by NDEs, has universal appeal to most human beings. The verifiable consistency across cultures, religions and belief of people who have near death experiences is remarkable. In most cases of NDE, the subject emerges with a renewed enthusiasm for life, respect for others and the absence of the fear of dying. However, not all NDEs are happy ones and there is no standard way of grading this experience for intensity, quality or authenticity. There is, however, clinical evidence that there are substantial biochemical changes that take place in the brain of those going through the pre-death processes. The drop in blood pressure and reduction of oxygen reaching the brain result in the secretion of certain neurochemicals, which induce the classical 'dark tunnel' and then the 'tunnel of light' experience. Astronauts and others who are subjected to negative G-forces have also occasionally reported similar 'tunnel of light' experiences. Even 'objective' researchers of such phenomena admit the inconclusive relationship between a Near Death Experience and what lies beyond death. Yet they often admit in private that they would like to believe in life after death. However, interest in paranormal phenomena is likely to fade away in the light of inner spiritual beauty and joy. The depth and boundlessness of pure consciousness supersedes all other consciousness and human experiences, including magic and miracles.

6.5 Preparing For Death

When all dualities unite and otherness merges into oneness, then death will be seen as simply transcending every movement and change to eternal perfection. The desire for prolonged life is a natural emotion justified logically to understand the true meaning and purpose of life before transfer to the next world. For thousands of years, cultures, civilisations and religions gave death its due importance and much of life was considered a preparation for the journey to the hereafter. Jalaluddin Rumi (the great Sufi saint and poet of the thirteenth century) visualised the processes of birth and death beautifully when he wrote: 'I died as a mineral and was born a plant. Then the plant died to be born as an animal and then the animal died so that the human is born. When the human in me dies, I shall metamorphose as an eternal soul'. Yesterday died to give birth to today and so today will lead to a new tomorrow. Every creation is part of the whole process of beginning-and-end and the recurring cycle of emanation and return.

> ....and (so) lend to Allah a goodly loan. Whatever good you send ahead it is for your selves, you will find with Allah, something greater and better. And seek forgiveness from Allah. Allah is Forgiving, Merciful. (73:20)

How does one prepare optimally for death and the next realm? A human being's life is given meaning by its association and relationships to activities and other creations. We can only see ourselves through the eyes and minds of others. Consequently, whoever gives and serves others more will experience a richer and fuller life, larger than the individual self and beyond one's conditioned consciousness. Imam Ali had said 'After death, nothing will suffice you except your good deeds which you have forwarded. Therefore, live for pious and good deeds.'

It is said that the thrill of the wise one is in seeing inner sameness, in essence, veiled in outer differences. Self-acceptance relates to understanding others and seeing sameness in otherness. Whoever glimpses the brilliant flashes of light from the soul is nearer to the discovery that a human being is more than the sum total of all roles or activities; one is, in essence, a sacred soul that reflects all the glories of the one magnificent God.

> By no means will you attain righteousness until you spend on others out of what you cherish yourselves; and whatever you spend, Allah surely knows it. (3:92)

The religion of Islam is founded upon self-awareness, responsibility and acting virtuously in preparation and readiness for the next life. The most frequent remedy the Prophet gave in preparation for death was generosity with what one likes to keep and understanding the fickle nature of this world, thus engendering love for the next life that is free from human injustice and mischief. The Prophet also taught that for a spiritually wise person the least important issue in this world is material poverty or the fear of darkness in the grave.

> It is prescribed upon you, when death approaches any of you, and if he has wealth to leave, that he makes a will in favour of his parents and relatives, correctly and fairly. (This is) a duty upon the pious. (2:180)

Imam Ali said: 'You (now) and the doomsday are in the same period (already here); it looks like it had come with jolts and settled down on earth and the world was swept away along with its living creatures, and the cry (the shock) has pulled them out of graves.' Space and time are relative and are important only to us who are immersed in the so-called 'real' physical world. Truth is timeless. Multiples vanish as Oneness appears. Falsehood disappears in the light of truth.

Imam Ali also said, 'Surely Allah is the glorified, the sublime, nothing is hidden from Him. He knows what people do in the nights and the days. He knows all the details and His knowledge covers all that exists. Your limbs are witnesses, your organs are His soldiers, the 'selves' are like His watching eyes and everything is open to Him.' He reminds us that, 'When a person reads his records on doomsday, all past actions appear as though they had happened a moment ago and Allah will enable one to recall every movement, minute by minute'.

...........and take a provision for the journey, you should know that the best of provision is piety, So fear Me, O you men of understanding! (2:197)

There is no repentance for those who go on doing evil deeds, until death comes to them, and they say: "Now I repent"; nor (for) those who die while they are unbelievers. For such people We have prepared a painful punishment. (4:18)

The Qur'an mentions the repentance of the Pharaoh of Moses and preservation of his body:

Now! (you believe) while you refused to believe before, and you were one of the evil-doers - So this day We shall preserve your (dead) body that you may be a sign to those who come after you! And there are many among mankind who are heedless of Our signs. (10:91-92)

It is interesting that the body of the Pharaoh of Moses is preserved to this day and is occasionally given a world tour in a special container – after some 32 centuries.

Someone asked the Prophet what was the best preparation for the next life. He replied, 'Performing obligations, keeping from forbidden things and then do not care whether death falls on you or you fall upon death.'

Regarding the two angels who record deeds and the angel of death, the Prophet said, 'Allah appoints two angels who keep on recording good and bad deeds. As death approaches, the two angels leave one alone and there comes the angel of death to take the soul out. When the body is put in the grave, the soul is released from its earthly bondage. Then the angels will ask questions and after a while they leave. At the time of doom, both angels of the good and bad deeds meet people and place records of their deeds upon their necks. One will be his driver to the assembling place and the second will be his witness.' The Qur'an mentions:

If only you could see when the angels take back those who disbelieve (at death), slashing their faces and their backs, and (saying): Taste the punishment of burning. (8:50)

No, indeed, when (the soul) reaches the collar bone – And it will be said: "Who can cure him and save him from death?" – And he (the dying person) will know that it is (the time) of final parting; - And one leg will be twisted around the other leg (resisting death) - On that Day, the drive will be to your Lord! (75:26-30)

Regarding the time of death the Prophet said, 'I have seen some very strange things, which I would like to share with you. I saw a man from my people and the angel of death was approaching him but his care for his parents delayed his departure. I saw a person engulfed in the wrath of Allah; his ablution came and saved him. I saw a person surrounded by some wicked beings, then he remembered God and that saved him.' The Prophet also mentioned that in the same way as we pray for the deceased and wish them an easy journey, the dead also try to reciprocate. This does not mean that the deceased or those who are living can always affect each other at will or reliably, however, those who believe that the dead can influence them positively may derive some benefit from this belief.

6.6 Ease and Difficulty

Imam Ali said: 'servants of God, for those who have not repented during their lifetime, after death the torment is worse than the agony of death. Be afraid of its narrowness, darkness and loneliness. And "loss" to which Allah has referred is the chastisement of the grave.'

Freedom after death implies freedom from worldly afflictions, attachments and desires. Muslim scholars describe the souls of the virtuous exulting in liberation from this temporal world; they will delight in their ability to roam freely through the infinite. Life on this earth is concerned mostly with the limited, visible physical reality. On the other hand, the souls of the virtuous know no limitations as they continue their heavenly journey, each in accordance with its rank advances to its specific stations and level. In paradise they will recognize that the beauty and attractions of the earthly world was trivial in comparison with the beauty and bliss of paradise. The Qur'an promises that the righteous will enjoy the company and fellowship of God's chosen elite. This companionship is a source of great joy and celebration for the virtuous.

They will never taste death except the first death (of this world), and He will save them from the torment of the blazing Fire, (44:56)

Although the shape or image of people in the hereafter may in general resemble the bodily form they had in this world, certain differences will also be apparent because inner personal attributes will appear externally. Thus, the spiritual light or inner darkness of an individual in this world will become clearly visible in the hereafter.

There are numerous issues and questions that most people seek answers to, irrespective of different cultures or religious faiths. One major concern is the way justice is meted out in this world as well as the hereafter. Where is divine mercy in violence and wars that cause millions to suffer? What are the causes? Are accidents, premature death and similar unexpected events punishments? Why is it that nature seems to afflict mostly the poor people and spare the rich? What should our relationship be with animals and plants? To what extent is the human being a steward or God's representative on earth? Will a cremated person be resurrected? What can one do to reduce one's guilt for wrong actions or abuse? What can one do for a departed person to whom one has been unjust and so on? Our needs and desires to know are often a prelude to openings in higher consciousness. Personal ignorance knocks on the door of Divine knowledge and thus, the self will receive insights from its soul.

These numerous questions can only be understood, if we remember the basic models of life's consciousness. Sentiency and animation are the foundations for life's experiences and are energised by the forces for survival and growth. With human beings, a higher power of consciousness brings about the quest for what is eternal, perfect or Divine. We can say that there are two complementary spheres of consciousness. One is a basis to life and produces conditioned or limited awareness and individuality. This power feeds the basic will to survive and grow and has no notion of morality or justice. The other is pure or universal consciousness that relates to the human soul or essence. The basic self or ego consciousness evolves towards the higher self or soul through reason, intellect and insights. The evolved mind is a prelude to the heart, which is the abode of the soul and the sacred presence. It is the advent of higher consciousness that enables man to seek virtues, morality, justice and truth.

Mankind was one people (basically simple) and then we sent prophets to bring good news and warning. (2:213)

The earth is like a laboratory for learning and experimenting on limited scales which are samples of patterns and light fields in the realm of the unseen. We are given the chance to experience justice and other perfections on limited levels as samples of the universal perfections and balances, which are etched within the human soul. With wisdom and reflection, we begin to realise that the self or ego is the earthly shadow of the sacred soul and desires all the great qualities which are inherent within the soul, which reflects the original sacred light. All earthly experiences and challenges to the self need to be dealt with as an exercise of relating the inner and outer aspects of our human nature.

87

Spiritual awakening is to do with unison between self and soul, which evolves us to have the sight as well as the insight to understand many of life's paradoxes and complex issues. We are here on earth to grow in perception and intuition to be ready to return to the realm of pure consciousness and absolute truth after death.

In this way God makes clear to you His messages, so that you might [learn to] use your reason. (2:242)

Spiritual evolvement and growth implies taking reason and logic to its utmost limit and then waiting for intuition or insights. Good preparation for death requires the practice of this process. When you are about to relocate to another town, you wish to minimize the shock of uncertainties by preparing as well as you can and then to trust and have good expectations. This is why it is often said: by trust, faith and good expectation of God, you will come to realise and witness the best outcome.

BURIALS AND GRAVES

The human body is the worldly abode of the sacred soul and, therefore, deserves respect and care. As such, when it is time for the soul to return to its light source and the body to its earthly origin, both must be remembered and treated with respect. Different cultures follow different practices in the process of burial. The Abrahamic religions share some rituals and ways of reverence for the deceased. The Islamic practices of burial of the deceased body show care and respect for the living too by safeguarding against the sight of the disintegration of the body. Islam recommends the attendance of funerals and the regular visiting of graves as a sign of respect and a reminder of human destiny.

7.1 Respect for Body and Soul

The Qur'an emphasises the sacredness of human life by saying that whoever kills another human being (not just as punishment), it is as though he had slain all mankind; whereas, if anyone saves a life, it shall be as though he has saved the lives of all mankind.

Whilst alive, every human being likes to be respected, acknowledged and affirmed. This is rooted in the fact that the soul is divinely ordained and acknowledged. Thus, the person who is alive because of the soul will also desire the same values for the self or ego, with its physical identity. The self-soul dual nature within us causes countless paradoxes in behaviour and desires. At the end, the soul triumphs and continues its journey of return to its sacred Source.

Our respect for the dead body is a simple acknowledgment of the sacredness of the soul which had inhabited it for a while. Since every soul is sacred, then every human being deserves respect and equity. An individual with soul consciousness and respect for other souls will experience reciprocation from others. The outer world always mirrors the inner. Self-respect, concern, awareness, appropriate relationship and harmony with others are necessary steps for deeper awareness of the divine presence within the human heart.

> Those of you who believe! You are only responsible for yourselves, the misguided cannot hurt you when you are on the right path; you will return to Allah, and He will inform you of what you were doing. (5:105)

7.2 Courtesies and Ceremonies

Imam Ali had said: 'Death is of three kinds: good news of permanent blessings; bad news of permanent chastisement; depression and anxiety.' During a person's death, all those who are present must maintain the utmost of respect, courtesy and reverent attention. The process of death is a major event for the dying and the living. We must therefore allow nature to take its course peacefully and gracefully. The atmosphere must be calm and without outbursts of emotionality, agitation or self-pity. Whenever possible, appropriate religious chanting or reading of Qur'an may add calmness and dignity to the eventful day. The Qur'anic reference to Jesus is a lofty state desired by many:

> Hence, peace was upon him on the day when he was born, and on the day of his death, and. will be [upon him] on the day when he shall be raised (again) to life. (19:15)

As one dies, numerous human faculties shut down: hearing, sight and other senses fade and the mind may review past events through blurred flashes. There is often some inner turmoil until the self (ego and mind) is prepared and has readied itself for departure. Relevant prayers for the dead, expression of grief and respectful remembrance are all helpful to those affected by the death. Prayers for and charitable giving on behalf of the dead make the participant feel good and adds grace to the occasion. It is said that the spiritual vitality and condition of a people can be gauged by their conduct during the process of dying and relationship with the dead, their graves and their cemeteries.

Those (who) the angels cause to die are in a good state, (the angels will be) saying: Peace be on you: enter the garden for what you did. (16:32)

7.3 Burial Ritual
The process of washing, shrouding, praying, holding a funeral and public participation in the burial is a common custom in many religions. In Islam, the burial of the dead is the last religious ritual. The body is first bathed facing the *Ka'bah* (Mecca). Usually the body is washed three times, the first in 'sidr' (beri) leaves, then in water mixed with camphor and the third time in pure water. Once bathed, the dead person is shrouded, usually in three cloths – two sheets and the third a shirt. Just after shrouding, a ceremonial prayer is offered for the soul of the deceased, attendance of which is obligatory for those present. The prayer consists of five announcements (*takbirat* – the declaration that God is greater: *Allahu Akbar*) and four supplications in between. Thereafter, the funeral can commence.

Usually a dead body is buried in a pit the depth of a man's height and spacious enough for laying down the body. It is recommended that the depth of the grave not to be deeper than 'three hands deep' (i.e. from shoulder joint to tip of middle finger). The body must be laid down respectfully and three or four men (preferably; including a son) climb down into the pit for this purpose. Then, the basic Islamic confirmation, that there is no god other than Allah and that Muhammad is His Prophet, is recited inside the grave. It is customary also that the grave should be covered with its own soil remnants and no additional earth should be brought in from another location.

The Prophet had mentioned that: 'Allah has commanded the burial of the deceased in order to prevent the bad effects of its disintegration (its awful outer condition and smell) so that the living should not feel upset and discomforted by it. God has ordered entombment for keeping the deceased hidden from friends as well as enemies so that there is neither pleasure nor sorrow with regards to the decaying body.'

The Prophet Muhammad advised: 'Take the deceased to the grave quickly and recite the first few verses of *Surah al-Baqarah* (the 2nd Surat) near his head and recite the last verses of the same chapter near his feet.' He also forbade burial by night except in special cases in which it would be better for the deceased.

Funeral attendance is considered preferential to a wedding. If both occasions occur at the same time, then attending a funeral takes precedence as it reminds us of our own death, whereas a wedding is a distraction from this important event. In a funeral, you are expected to look sad. In a wedding, you are expected to be happy. Yet the wedding is a temporary and uncertain state in our life, whilst death is the ultimate destiny for all. It had been a Sufi tradition that the day of the teacher's death is regarded as their wedding or *urs*: the man weddings are an earthly attempt for union and complementarity whereas the return of soul to its Creator is the ultimate and perfect wedding. Until now many Sufi centres commemorate annually the *urs* of their deceased master.

The Prophet reminds us to attend every funeral as though it is one's own. The more we visualise death and place ourselves metaphorically or physically in a grave, the more likely that our worldly worries and attachments become less dominant. He also directed Muslims to attend with peace and moderation and to keep thinking about the event, whilst remembering their similar fate in the future. At our present time, there is a growing interest and understanding in the important process of grief and bereavement – this is reflected within popular literature, partly in an attempt to break down social taboos that have developed around the issue of death.

The practice of burying the dead varies according to religion and culture. Ceremonies and procedures for taking the dead body to the grave also vary considerably, even in the same religion. However, within the Abrahamic traditions (Judaism, Christianity and Islam), there are many similarities, especially with regard to honour and respect for the departed and care for graves and burial sites.

Sensitive or intuitive visitors to graves sometimes pick up certain feelings or messages from the dead. Human beings are very complex entities and can have the potential to pick up subtle energies from where the body had been left. These feelings could explain why some graves are visited often and become points of pilgrimage. The spiritual atmosphere that prevails in many places of worship can also prevail at some tombs, mausoleums or graves. This atmosphere helps the living visitors to connect with higher states of awareness and thereby enhance their own spiritual sensitivity. Until recently in the Muslim world, most towns and cities were built around one or more saintly tombs. Towns were frequently named after the local patron saint.

Pilgrimage to tombs of prophets, saints or special sites known for their healing powers have been part of human behaviour from ancient times. Due to the intention of the visitors and their mental preparedness, miracles or unusual experiences can sometimes occur. The more a person has faith or trust in God, and the soul of the deceased as a link to God, the greater the likelihood of receiving an inspiration, insight or an answer to prayers from the unseen. The Qur'an addresses the righteous whose self is subdued and trusts in God:

"O contented self (at peace) return to your Lord well pleased and pleasing (Him): enter together with my other servants, enter my Paradise!" (89: 27-30)

In Islam, a funeral is an important event for all concerned. We are advised to attend not only the funeral of our relatives but also that of unknown Muslims as well as others. The Prophet said, 'The first way a dead believer benefits others is that he prays to God to forgive all those who attended his funeral.' Therefore, it is considered obligatory for the close relatives of the deceased to inform other people of the death so that they might attend the prayer for the dead as well as the funeral. Condolences are recommended mainly at the graveside and not later, although many communities hold gatherings for condolence and remembrance. It is painful to realise illusions and go past them to the realms of higher consciousness and truth. You need courage, passion for truth and divine grace.

The Prophet said: 'Being able to weep is a mercy but screaming is from Satan.' He also said 'I do not prevent people from weeping but I prevent them from wailing on the dead. He forbade the slapping or beating of the face, tearing garments and screaming.' The scholars of Islam corroborate this by claiming that weeping over the death of a loved one is allowed but excessive crying, tearing garments, pulling hair, hitting the body with knives and chains and uttering words against providence or God are all forbidden.

A burial visibly confirms the absence of a person from the worldly realm and shows respect for the physical remains of the dead. It is a clear closure to the deceased's life and an irrevocable message to his family and companions. By interring the body away from plain view, the pain of loss will soon recede and be lessened. Some cultures go through much effort to prevent the decay of the body, such as embalming. Mummification is an extreme form of embalming further retarding the decaying process. Burial in a shroud or coffin also slows down the decomposition process.

And in the end He causes him to die and brings him to the grave; (80:21)

Respect for the deceased has been practiced amongst humankind from time immemorial. In some cultures, it is customary to dress the deceased in fine or ceremonial garb. Many consider that the deceased should look his or her best. The practice of including grave goods served several purposes in various older cultures, who believed that certain objects or items were necessary for entrance into the afterlife.

In ancient Jewish culture, a natural cave enlarged and adapted by excavation was the standard type of sepulchre. Some of these were in gardens, by roadsides and even adjoining houses. The growth in urban populations soon required that cemeteries be located away from city centres.

Body positioning is often another important aspect of the burial ritual. In Christianity, for example, one finds the practice of extended burial prevalent (fully extending the body with arms straight down the sides or folded across the chest with legs kept straight). In other rites, one finds the body put into a flexed position with legs bent or crouched. Positioning of the body reflects the mark of respect for the dead accorded by that particular culture.

Grave markings, tomb coverings or mausoleums are human attempts to reflect the soul's immortality and express respect for the dead. Most modern cultures mark the location of the body with a headstone, at the very least. This serves two purposes: firstly, graves will not be accidentally exhumed and secondly, the headstone often contains information and tribute to the deceased. This remembrance is a part of the offering of the loved ones of the deceased. Some fundamentalist Muslims forbid any grave-marking and deplore this practice. One reason given is the extreme behaviour of some visitors to graves, which appears as grave worship.

7.4 Praying for the Departed

The Prophet commanded doing good to one's living or dead

parents. He said: 'perform prayer, keep fasts, and give charity on their behalf, for it will benefit both you and them. God will reward you for your good deeds.'

One can pray for several dead people at the same time. When asked about the benefit of prayers for the dead, the Prophet said that Allah would make the grave feel wide due to the prayer and make the dead know that ease is due to the prayer. He was then asked if one could include one more person in that prayer and the reply was yes.

We are told that the dead feel the prayers and charity of the living and will feel comfort and pleasure if mercy and repentance is asked for him. It is like sending a gift to one's friend. If someone performs prayer, keeps the fast, makes a pilgrimage, spends money and does good deeds in the name of the dead, all these acts reach the deceased and will be included in the record of the performer, as well as the dead.

Imam Ali said: 'Visit the graves of your deceased people because they derive pleasure from it. It is better to ask Allah to fulfil your needs at the grave of your father or mother besides praying for them also.' Muslims often visit graves on Thursdays or Fridays and commemorate the fortieth day after death and the yearly cycle.

Regarding the soul's exposure to the good and bad deeds of the living, we are told that the soul of every believer visits its relatives and their good deeds are shown to them, while bad deeds are hidden from them. Likewise, the souls of unbelievers visit relatives but their bad deeds only are shown to them whilst their good deeds are hidden from them. Such visits are said to be often at sunset.

The desire to connect with the dead, either to acquire some idea about the hereafter, to appease the anger of ancestors or reduce personal guilt is common to most human beings. In primitive religions, connection with ancestors is a cornerstone of worship. Islam frowns upon excessive interference with, and expectations from, the dead.

THE NEW REALM

The development of higher consciousness in this world is a preparatory prelude to a smooth entry into the hereafter. The degree to which the self has been aligned with the soul will determine the ease with which one continues the journey into the next phase. Faith, trust in God, good deeds, transformative worship, purity of heart and all other religious acts doubtlessly make the transition less shocking for all.

Upward mobility seems a natural tendency for all living entities on earth, as well as after death. Some million years ago, plants and animals spilled out of the oceans onto land. Then, from the carboniferous forest, living entities (future birds) took off to air. The upward movement of plants towards light seemed a prelude to flying further up into the air. Spores and seeds spreading out seemed to initiate the act of flying. The soul too, after death, soars higher within the subtler realms of pure consciousness and sacred space.

> Were We then exhausted with the first creation? No, yet they are in confused doubt about a new creation (Resurrection). (50:15)

8.1 The Hereafter

During life on earth, personal conditioned consciousness changes or evolves according to one's intentions and actions. After death, there is no freedom of will or action. In this new situation, all souls (with their earthly self/ego) observe and experience the new realities and states of the hereafter. In a way, when asleep we have no clear choice regarding our dreams. The world of the hereafter is like a new type of prolonged dream until the end of all creation.

The new experience and awareness is restricted and blurred, yet the deceased person continues to experience both agreeable and disagreeable states. When one is prepared for, and reconciled with, the advent of death well before its occurrence, then there is a predominating agreeable drift into this new world. It is a great shock for anyone to lose all the senses and the power of thinking, acting or being in control of one's situation. It is a good practice for the living to visualise being stripped of all normal possibilities of action or behaviour. To befriend death, occasionally withdraw and abstain from what is considered normal daily life. This is a great exercise that enables us to face death with ease. Death is involuntary total submission; the more we practice voluntary abandonment of thoughts and actions, the better prepared we will be for this world and the hereafter. Meditation, prayers and all practices that help transcendence are of great assistance. A few Sufi masters used the practice of lying down in a prepared grave before actual death with cheerful readiness.

> And if you (O Muhammad) wonder (at people's lack of faith) then you will find it incredible when they pray: "When we are dust (how can), we indeed then be (raised) in a new creation…"13:5)

Death will affect the function of hearing, sight and speech. It is interesting to note that hearing which is considered the earliest sense to develop in the womb is the last to go. As death takes over, then all faculties will be lost and the soul will depart from the body, often with a sigh.

Due to the soul's familiarity and long-term connection with the body and mind, the shock of death will take its toll during the transition to the new situation. To reconcile and accept what is happening may take minutes, hours, or longer. In some cases, the turmoil may never cease – that is hell. This is where the soul is heavily weighed down by the ego/self and its attachment to worldly matters. This is the case with ghosts and other strange phenomena associated with dead persons' burdened souls – they refuse to depart from the earthly state.

With death the brain ceases to function; the five senses and other faculties are lost but replaced by a new and different sense of awareness that is beyond our worldly grasp. Past attachments, unfinished worldly business and lack of familiarity with the new dreamlike state are all causes for difficulties and need for adjustment after death. This is why it is thought that the soul hovers around the grave for a while. There are usually some cyclical patterns of the deceased soul visiting or being close to the grave or to the loved ones left behind. The most frequently mentioned cycles are: three days, five days, a week, forty days and one year, or annually, after death.

After death, the worldly personality, identity and all normal mental activities will disappear and will be superseded by a new way of feeling and experiencing life. All previous worldly concerns, values, images and understanding as well as all personal, social and religious issues have now vanished and are replaced with an entirely new dreamlike situation which is more real and enduring.

> And certainly the reward of the hereafter is much better for those who believe (in divine unity) and are in continuous awareness. (12:57)

Religious or pious people who practice and live their faith are more likely to reconcile with death and face the experience more peacefully and with ease. To understand and love God's qualities and attributes will make the transition, to the hereafter, easier. Also, better understanding of the illusory world and its distractions will make departure a welcome event. Acceptance of God as the source of all connections and unification in existence, makes it natural for us to respond to the divine spark—the soul—within our heart. Ultimately, it is due to God's mercy and grace that we are saved from the earthly confines.

The Prophet Muhammad said: 'When the believer dies the graveyards decorate themselves and every place wishes to be his burial place. But, when an unbeliever dies, the cemetery becomes dark, so as not to allow the person to be buried over there.'

Experiences in the Grave

From what thing did He create him? From a drop of sperm; He created him, then He made him according to (perfect) measure. Then He made the path (of growth) easy (for him). Then He causes him to die, then assigns to him a grave. (80:18-21)

Suffering or joy start right from the time of burial. A number of Qur'anic verses describe death and its aftermath from different perspectives:

And who can be more unjust than he who invents a lie against Allah ... and if you could only see the wrongdoers when they are in the agonies of death, while the angels are stretching out their hands (saying): "Deliver your souls (save your selves)! This day you will be repaid with the torment of degradation for saying something other than the truth about Allah. And you rejected His signs with disrespect! (haughtiness)" (6:93)

As for those the angels take in death who are unjust to themselves, they will offer (false) submission: (and say): "We did not do any evil". Oh yes you did! Allah knows what you did. (16:28)

And when death overtakes one of them he says: Send me back my Lord so that I may do good... (23:99-100)

As for those whom the angels take (in death) who are unjust to themselves, the (angels) say (to them): "In what (condition) were you?" They reply: "We were oppressed on earth." They (angels) say: "Was the earth of Allah not spacious enough for you to emigrate?" Such men will find their abode in Hell - What an evil destination! (4:97)

Enter the gates of hell, remaining there forever; how evil is the dwelling place of the haughty – And it is said to those who guard themselves (against evil): What is it that your Lord has revealed? They say, goodness. For those who do good in this world, there is good, and certainly the abode of the hereafter is better; and certainly most excellent is the abode of those who guard themselves (against evil); (16:29-30)

... Surely, they have been in despair to receive any good in the Hereafter, just as the disbelievers have been in despair about those (buried) in graves. (60:13)

These verses show that people in graves have some kind of consciousness and they feel chastisement or blessings. In Chapter *Surah al-Yasin* (36:28-67), we are given a serious picture of the power of God regarding life and death of people and civilisations, the resurrection, evaluation of deeds, hell and paradise. These verses challenge the doubtful minds to reflect and consider the revealed scenes. The Prophet said: 'The grave is the first step of the next life; if one gets salvation at this level the next stage is easier.'

The Garden and The Fire

The gates to paradise are wide open for everyone but you cannot enter until you are guided by the divine light from your heart. Then, you actually realise yourself to be on the other side of the gate already in the garden.

It is He Who sends down manifest signs to His servant that He may bring you out from darkness into light. And certainly, Allah is to you full of kindness, Most Merciful. (57:9)

Allah is the guardian of those who believe. He brings them out of the darkness into the light; and (as to) those who disbelieve, their guardians are Shaitans who take them out of the light into the darkness; they are the inmates of the fire, in it they shall abide. (2:257)

... and Allah invites to the garden and to forgiveness by His permission, and makes clear His signs to people, so that they may be mindful.(2:221)

The Qur'an, the book of signs and allegories, describes paradise as a garden with flora and fauna in abundant varieties to satisfy any desire or need. There are two lakes that flow, two kinds of each fruit will be there, people will be at great comfort and ease in paradise where the trees are heavily laden with fruits. There are two (levels of) gardens and two springs are gushing out of them. There are trees of palm, pomegranates and other fruits in plethora. In paradise, there are beautiful, well-mannered and chaste women (perfect partners) and neither humans nor *Jinns* have ever contaminated their purity. The people in paradise will be wearing green garments, precious and well decorated – a state of ultimate luxury and contentment.

The description of different aspects of hell and paradise cover several hundred verses in the Qur'an. Life on earth is described as a sample of the hereafter and the 'state' of the garden and that of hell has already been partially experienced on earth.

And the garden will be brought near to those who guard themselves (against evil), it will not be far off: This is what you were promised, this is for every one who turns frequently (to Allah), keeps (His limits); Who feared the Beneficent in secret (with himself) and comes to Him with a penitent heart: Enter it in peace, this is the day of eternity. (50:31-34)

Also, the people in the garden hope to be elevated to a higher state in consciousness.

> O you who believe! Return to Allah with a sincere repentance; It maybe that your Lord will remove from you your bad actions and admit you into the gardens beneath which rivers flow, on the day that Allah will not disgrace the Prophet and those who believe with him; their light shall run on before them and on their right side; they will say: Lord! complete our light, and grant us cover over our faults. You are able to do any thing. (66:8)

The garden is described such that it is not definable by any space dimensions.

> And hasten to forgiveness from your Lord; and for a Garden, as wide as the heavens and the earth, prepared for those who guard themselves (against evil). (3:133)

The following are various descriptions of Hell:

> But those who disbelieve and deny Our signs such are the dwellers of the Fire, they shall live there forever. (2:39)

> They ask you to hasten the Punishment. And surely Hell will encompass the disbelievers. (29:54)

> And your Lord says: Call upon Me, I will answer you; surely those who are too proud for My service shall soon enter hell abased. (40:60)

> On the Day when they shall be dragged into the fire on their faces, [they will be told:] "Now taste the touch of hell-fire!" (54:48)

The Companions of the Left (those who are evil by nature), what will be the Companions of the Left? – (They will be) in the midst of a Fierce Blast of Fire and in Boiling Water – And in the shades of Black Smoke: - Nothing (will be there) to refresh, nor please (56:41-44)

About to enter a glowing fire, given to drink from a boiling spring. No food for them except the bitterness of dry thorns, which gives no strength and neither stills hunger. (88:4-7).

Surely the tree of the Zaqqum, (deadly tree) – Is the food of the sinful – Like molten brass; it will boil in their bellies – Like the boiling of hot water. (44:43-46).

We need to remember that as human beings we are conditioned by our worldly minds, senses, body, intellect and other organs which are all earthly and definable. The new realm is not subject to time or space, as such, and only has a hint of duality and worldly discernment. The so-called 'real world' of ours is based on perpetual emanation and return and the process of exchange between energy and matter in endless ways. We become accustomed to the processes of time and the dimensions of space from birth and can only relate all experiences to the four dimensions (three of space and one of time). Our imaginal faculty of discernment—between forms and meaning, the values we give to objects and feeling or thought, though worldly—bears resemblance to the hereafter. The people in the garden too describe their new experiences as reminders of those on earth;

Give the good news to those who believe and do good deeds, that they will have gardens in which rivers flow underneath; whenever they will be given some fruit, they will say: This is what was given to us before; but they were only given a like of it (but superior in taste), and they will have pure mates and they will remain there forever. (2:25)

We know that the condition after death is very different from our normal worldly experiences. Our world is based on binary roots (matter/anti-matter, yes/no) and the human challenge is to discover connections within dualities. The realm of after-death is of a different nature as it is based on a unitary stream with only faint shades of past dualities. The essence and state of the after-world is new and alien to the human psyche, whereas the soul is familiar with this domain. Thus, the more the self has practiced submission to the soul, the easier is the journey.

Generally, it is accepted in Islam that after death a person experiences confusion and bewilderment. The new life is experienced in strange ways, which we could never comprehend before. The perception of matter and energy is different from our sensations of the earthly world – they are inseparable. The provisions and needs, in this after-world, are totally different from those on earth. This new realm is based on subtle forces which are beyond normal mental understanding and are, therefore, referred to as divine grace, power or commands. New knowledge will occur when previous assumptions are removed with fresh insights. Darkness will be replaced with emerging light.

On the Day when every person will be confronted with all the good he has done, and all the evil he has done, he will wish that there were a great distance between him and his evil. And Allah warns you against Himself (His Punishment) and Allah is full of Kindness to the (His) servants. (3:30)

During life on earth, selfless acts, prayers, inner integrity, harmony, wellbeing and trust in the ever-perfect presence of God on earth and heavens are all great foundations for an easy journey into this *terra incognita*. All of our worldly intentions, actions and experiences give hints and clues to this new after-world. Our world is like the tip of the iceberg in relationship to the vast unseen realms. It does, however, present a sample of what is to come.

> And the Book will be set in place, then you will see the guilty fearing from what is in it, and they will say: Ah! woe to us! What is this book it does not omit either a small thing or a big thing, but records (everything); what they had done will be present (there); and your Lord does not deal unjustly with anyone. (18:49)

Angels and Jinn

> It is He Who sends His blessings on you, and (so do) His angels, that He may bring you forth out of utter darkness into the light; and He is Merciful to the believers. (33:43)

Our modern worldview is based mostly on scientific knowledge and provable facts. Souls, angels and jinn remain intangible entities, whose effect can be felt but they cannot be reliably defined, contained or categorised. The Qur'an has numerous references to angels and jinn, which were elaborated upon by the Prophet and his enlightened followers. In the Qur'an, there is a complete chapter entitled: *The Jinn*, describing them as similar to human beings regarding their vices and virtues as well as their social and community life. Angels can be regarded as energy bundles or souls that have no free will of their own but can assume forms on occasion and appear to persons with the appropriate receptivity. The essence of angels is light but modified and contained. Angels have no egos or individual personalities.

> Allah bears witness that there is no god but He, and (so do) the angels and those having knowledge, maintaining His creation with justice; there is no god but He, the All-Mighty, the All-Wise. (3:18)

It is He who appointed you (His) agents, inheritors of the earth and raised some of you above others in rank ...(6:165)

And to Allah prostrate all creatures that are in the heavens and all that are in the earth, and the angels, and they are not proud (to submit completely). (16:49)

The jinn have a fiery essence and are like the unseen shadowy version of human beings. They live in groups, have families and nations, procreate and behave or misbehave, as we do. They also live and die according to a different time-scale. The jinn normally do not interfere with human beings but much mischief can take place when there is an involvement as they begin to influence the human mind and other faculties. Jinn possession can occur when the human mind is receptive, or is weakened due to psychic or psychological disturbance.

O assembly of jinn and men! If you have power to pass beyond the zones of the heavens and the earth, then pass (them)! But you will never be able to pass them............ (55:33)

Angels and jinn have varying levels of power and abilities. The Qur'an and other religious references to the number and extent of angels' wings is a metaphor regarding the extent of their energy and power. The same principle relates to the size or power of jinn.

And the jinn He created from a smokeless flame of fire. (55:15)

Angels and jinn belong to the subtler unseen realm of creation where matter and physicality is not as 'hard' or 'stable' as humans experience on earth. We are made of clay or earth, activated by light and are referred to as middle people – we contain matter and energy, the earth and the heavens, we are caught in time as ego and body and yet timeless as a soul. We can understand both the quantum world as well as the outer physical realities. Heaven and earth meet within the human soul. Thus, we are a microcosm within the macrocosm.

And I created jinn and humankind only that they should worship Me (Alone). (51:56)

Worship implies knowledge and adoration of God's great qualities, such as immortality, power, wealth, knowledge and scores of other desirable traits. The human soul is engrained with all the divine qualities and the self is the shadow that loves these attributes and can only attain them by full submission and union with its soul.

COSMIC CATACLYSM AND RESURRECTION

And guard yourselves against a day in which you shall be returned to Allah.......... (2:281)

The next phase in the cosmic journey involves the collapse of the universe and the end of time and space as we experience it. This universal death is followed by a second creation, which follows the end of the earthly one, where separation of body from soul takes place. With this new phase, self and soul are once again reunited to witness the power and oneness that is behind creation. This event is often referred to as the resurrection. Within this phase is judgement of how we conducted our life and evolved during our earthly life; this includes the reading of our own records of mind and heart. In this second creation, although the body may have some hazy presence, it is the inner states which are more apparent. In our world, the outer form masks the inner and in this realm, the inner state appears more evident than the outer. The process of death is a mirror image of birth. In this life we rely on our senses and outer awareness. After death, it is the individual's state of evolved consciousness that matters.

9.1 Cataclysm

Whatsoever is on it (the earth) will perish. (55:26)

Whatever is born will die. Our universe too will come to an end. The individual microcosm and the celestial macrocosm reflect each other. In truth, all beginnings, ends and all the processes in between are only emanations from the ever-present Essence, which is not subject to change. The purpose of human consciousness is to yield, return and merge with the original, absolute and eternal Divine Light and Truth, which is the only lasting reality. We emanate from unity to experience duality and return by choice (faith and enlightenment) to the original Unity.

> Say: To whom belongs what is in the heavens and the earth? Say: To Allah; He has ordained mercy on Himself; most certainly He will gather you on the resurrection day— there is no doubt about it. (As for) those who have lost their souls, they will not believe. (6:12)

A time will come when a major cosmic shock, or collapse, will bring to an end all that has been living on earth, the underworld and elsewhere. Whatever is considered sentient or alive will die. This major event is like the mirror image of the emergence of creation or the big bang (as it is often called). This symmetry reflects a perfect emanation and return on a universal scale.

> ... Allah only tries you by this; and he will certainly make clear to you on the resurrection day that about which you differed. (16:92)

Every entity or whatever experiences individuality reflects an aspect of the original singularity. On earth, we use our mind or memory and then respond to the new experiences or perception. Near the end of time, awareness becomes more focused upon higher consciousness and cosmic unity rather than multiplicity and duality. The light of absolute unity that illumines consciousness and the soul becomes eminent.

The two cosmic blasts, or universal shocks, (trumpet blows as described in the Qur'an), heralds what is referred to as: the day of reckoning, doomsday, universal gathering or resurrection. The Qur'an uses numerous terms to refer to this event which heralds the ultimate universal destiny. Whatever was thought to be 'real' on earth will vanish from the scene and what emerges are the subtle energy fields that are interconnected and permeated by the unique light of God. This universal collapse of time-space signifies the end of everything discernable in existence; all dualities and outer forms or identities, earthly and heavenly. This unique process combines implosions and explosions interchangeably. It is the final end of all universes and realities and the beginning of a new state of transformation and resurrection, which signifies a return to source. Not easy to visualise or imagine clearly.

> And the earth will beam with the light of its Lord, and the Book will be laid down, and the prophets and the witnesses will be brought up, and judgment will be given between them with justice, and they will not be dealt with unjustly. (39:69)

9.2 The First Trumpet Blow

The Qur'an describes various aspects and events of the end of time through hundreds of verses referring to these momentous events starting with the first blow, or blast, which brings death to the whole universe. Then, comes a second blow for resurrection (new life), gatheredness and final accounts.

> And surely, the Hour is coming, there is no doubt about it, and certainly, Allah will resurrect those who are in the graves. (22:7)

The end of life on earth includes everything that is living or considered dead and brings to finality all cycles of births, deaths and all existences. The Qur'an describes resurrection as:

> And the Trumpet will be blown, and behold! From the graves they will come out quickly to their Lord. (36:51-52)

It is said that great earthquakes, eclipses and destructive winds are the signs of doomsday. The prophet counselled people that if they are still alive when the signs of doomsday appear, they should take refuge in mosques or places of worship.

The sun and moon are destined to collapse at an appointed moment:

> We created the heavens and the earth and all between them only for just ends, and for an Appointed Term: But those who reject Faith turn away from what they have been warned about. (46:3)

> Do you not see that Allah merges the night into the day (i.e. changes the number of the hours), and merges the day into the night, and has subjected the sun and the moon (to His laws), each running its course for an appointed term; and that Allah is All-Aware of what you do. (31:29)

> On the Day when the heaven will shake with a dreadful shaking, (52:9)

> [It will take place] on a Day when the sky will be like molten lead, (70:8)

> Then wait for the Day when the sky will bring forth a visible smoke. (44:10)

All of creation will perish and then will experience a new life again;

> It is He Who created you from clay, and then decreed a stated term (for you to live). And He has appointed another term for you to be resurrected, yet you doubt (in the Resurrection). (6:2)

> And (commanding you): "Seek the forgiveness of your Lord, and turn to Him in repentance, that He may grant you good life (with provisions) for an appointed term, (11:3)

Have they not seen that Allah Who created the heavens and the earth is able to create the like of them ... (17:99)

The universal destructions, collapses and ends are described in various ways:

When the sky splits open (84:1)

When heaven is split apart, it becomes red like oil [like molten lava] (55:37)

And the sky will be split apart, for that Day it will be very frail, (69:16)

When the sky is cleft asunder, (82:1)

And when the skies are opened and become [as wide-flung] gates; (78:19)

On that Day We will roll up the skies as written scrolls are rolled up; [and] as We brought into being the first creation, so We will produce a new one, a promise which We have undertaken: for, surely, We are able to do [all things]! (21:104)

They did not make a just estimate of Allah as is due to Him. And on the Day of Resurrection the whole of the earth will be grasped by His Hand and the heavens will be rolled up in His Right Hand. He is Glorified, and He is High above all that they associate as partners with Him! (39:67)

New heavens and earth:

On the Day when the earth will be changed to another earth and so will be the heavens, and they (all creatures) will appear before Allah, the One, the Irresistible. (14:48)

As mentioned previously, Judaism, Christianity and Islam have much in common regarding the description of the afterlife. Within the Christian belief of the afterlife is the idea that the universe will be consumed and nothing will be left. The present heaven and earth will be destroyed and a new heaven and earth will take their place. The visible coming of Christ in power and glory will be the signal for the rising of the dead (resurrection). All the dead who are to be judged will rise, the just and wicked alike, and they will rise with the bodies they had in life. This description is very similar to the Islamic view.

9.3 This World as a Metaphor for The Next

The mystery of life and human doubt or uncertainty about the origin of creation and its return can only be understood by faith and trust in regarding this world as a metaphor or sample to what is to come in the hereafter.

And he makes comparisons for Us, and forgets his own (origin and) creation. He says: "Who will give life to these bones when they have rotted away and became dust?" – Say: He will give life to them Who created them for the first time! And He is the All-Knower of every creation! (36:78-79)

Do they not consider that Allah, Who created the heavens and the earth, is able to create their like. (17:99)

And on the day when heaven will burst open with the clouds, and the angels will be sent down descending (in ranks) – The kingdom on that day will rightly belong to the Beneficent Allah, and it will be a hard day for the unbelievers (25:25-26)

It is He Who has created the heavens and the earth in truth, He is the All-Wise, Well-Aware.. (6:73)

And, the Day on which the Trumpet will be blown and all who are in the heavens and all who are on the earth, will be terrified except him whom Allah will (exempt). And all will come to Him humbled. (27:87)

9.4 Questioning and Judgment

[the earth] On that day shall tell her news – that your Lord had inspired her. (99:4-5)

In the new consciousness of the hereafter, all secrets and earthly realities will appear clearly and with no ambiguity.

The Prophet said, 'People will stumble on the Day of Judgment on four questions: How did you pass your life? How did you pass your adult age? How did you earn money and how did you spend it? And the love of my progeny'.

And We have made every man's actions to cling to his neck, and We will bring forth to him on the resurrection day a book which he will find wide open: "Read your book. Your own self is sufficient to take account against you this Day." (17:13-14)

Until they come to it, their ears and their eyes and their skins will bear witness against them as to what they did – And they will say to their skins: Why have you borne witness against us? They will say: Allah Who makes everything speak has made us speak, and He created you in the first place, and you will be brought back to Him – And you did not think to veil yourselves from your hearing, sight and skin testifying against you, but you thought that Allah would never know much of what you did – And it is that thought which you had about your Lord that has destroyed you, so now find yourself among the lost. (41:20-23)

In the new state people will not be able to speak but hands will talk, feet will become witnesses, skin will reveal deeds and nothing remains hidden.

The account and records of people will be given to the right hand of the righteous people and to the left hand of transgressors:

Then, as for him who will be given his Record in his right hand – He surely will receive an easy reckoning. (84:7-8)

Then as for him who is given his book in his right hand, he will say: Read my book: (69:19)

People of the left-hand side are now in darkness and hell.

The Companions of the Left, what will be the Companions of the Left? – In hot wind and boiling water – And the shade of black smoke – Neither cool nor refreshing – Verily, before that, they indulged in luxury – And they persisted in the great sin (Kufur) – And they used to say: "When we die and become dust and bones, are we then to be resurrected? - "as well as our forefathers?" - Say (Yes), those of old, and those of later times. (56:41-49)

But as for him who will be given his Record in his left hand, he will say: "I wish that I had not been given my Record! —"And that I had never known, how my Account is? —"I wish, that it had been my end (death)! —"My power and arguments (to defend myself) have gone from me!" —Lay hold on him, then put a chain on him, —Then throw him in the blazing Fire. — "Then fasten him with a chain whose length is seventy cubits!" —Surely, He did not believe in Allah, the Most Great, —Nor did he urge the feeding of the poor—So he has no friend here this Day, —Nor any food except filth , (69:25-36).

But whosoever is given his Record behind his back, —He will cry out for (his own) destruction, —And will enter a blazing Fire, and will be made to taste its burning. —he was among his people in joy! —he thought that he would never come back (to Us)! —Yes! his Lord has been ever watchful of him! (84:10-15)

At length, when they reach the (Fire), their ears and their eyes and their skins will bear witness against them as to what they did.— And they will say to their skins: Why do you testify against us? They shall say: Allah Who makes everything speak has made us speak, and He created you at first, and to Him you will be brought back. (41:20-21).

People of the right hand will rejoice:

Then as for him who will be given his Record in his right hand will say: "Here, read my Record! —"Surely, I knew that I would meet my Account!" —So he shall be in a life, well-pleasing. —In a lofty Paradise, —The fruits of which will be low and near at hand—Eat and drink pleasantly for what you did beforehand in the days gone by. —But as for him who will be given his Record in his left hand, he will say: "I wish that I had not been given my Record! (69:19-25)

Some faces will be bright with happiness on that Day, laughing and rejoicing. And some faces will be covered with dust and darkness on that Day. (80:38-41).

Our Lord! it is You Who will gather mankind together on the Day about which there is no doubt. Verily, Allah never breaks His Promise". (3:9)

The two cataclysmic shocks of doomsday and resurrection are described in more than seventy variations, all symbolising the end of known ways of life and the return to the original state of singularity and oneness. A dozen or so names are mentioned in the Qur'an to describe the day of judgement, day of account and the day of religion.

9.5 Resurrection

Isn't He, Who created the heavens and the earth able to create their like? Yes, indeed! He is the All-Knowing Supreme Creator—His Command, when He intends a thing, is only that He says to it, "Be!" and it is! —Therefore glory be to Him in Whose hand is the kingdom of all things, and to Him you shall be brought back. (36:81-83)

Say: "Travel in the land and see how (Allah) originated creation, and then Allah will bring forth (resurrect) the creation of the Hereafter. Allah is able to do all things." (29:20)

A provision for (Allah's) servants. And by it (water) We give life thereby to a dead land. Thus will be the resurrection [of the dead]. (50:11)

And the Trumpet will be blown, that will be the Day of the warning [promised for Resurrection]. (50:20-21)

Resurrection implies unison between self and soul in the presence of the cosmic soul. There are no longer beginnings or ends, for now is the phase of drift towards eternity. This universal gatheredness of all creation takes place in a new unique state where matters, energies, bodies and souls are united. Every person will carry some memory regarding the previous life and the extent of evolvement in consciousness. Past intentions, actions and thoughts become unified and are self-revealing, without any secrets, barriers or veils. Whilst living on earth, the most obvious part of a human being is the body; whereas the soul or inner intention is unseen. Now, self and soul will appear clearly and the shape of body as a vague haze. This state is the beginning of the new creation.

With the second blast, the dead will resurrect, come out of their graves and rush towards the assembling place:

The Day when they will hear the awful shout in truth, that will be the Day of coming out (from the graves (i.e. Resurrection) (50:42)

The Day when they will come out of the graves quickly as though racing to a goal, (70:43)

So withdraw from them. The Day that the Caller will call (them) to a terrible thing—They will come forth, with humbled eyes from (their) graves as if they were locusts spread abroad— Hastening towards the Caller, the disbelievers will say: "This is a hard Day." (54:6-8)

The Day on which We will gather those who guard (against evil) to the Beneficent Allah to receive honours. (19:85)

In the Abrahamic religions, this event is described in various allegorical or metaphorical ways with a strong tint of the relevant culture of different societies. Scholars and interpreters will invariably add their own colour to make this strange event imaginable by the public. Even before the advent of formal religion, ancient humans had imagined the idea of life's journey after death and resurrection. Essentially, resurrection signifies the ultimate connection between beginnings and ends, the outer and inner, meaning and form and what is seen and unseen.

The key factor in the story of resurrection is the noticeable Divine presence over all of creation, including angels, other entities and energy fields. Frequent questions about the end of life and resurrection are anticipated and answered in the Qur'an such as:

> Does man [a disbeliever] think that We can not assemble his
> bones? — Yes, We are Able to put together in perfect order (even)
> the tips of his fingers [his finger prints !] (75:3-4)

> And they used to say: What! when we die and have become dust
> and bones, shall we then indeed be raised?— "And also our
> forefathers?" — Say: "(Yes) verily, those of old, and those of later
> times—Shall most surely be gathered together for the appointed
> hour of a known day. (56:47-50)

Questions regarding body and soul resurrection are answered by
Allah's decree that he created us from dust, to dust we shall
return and from dust shall we be called out:

> From (the earth) We created you, and into it We will send you
> back, and from it We will bring you out once again. (20:55)

> And Allah has made you grow out of the earth as a growth:
> Afterwards He will return you into it (the earth), and bring you
> forth (again on the Day of Resurrection)? (71:17-18)

> He said: "There you will live, and there you will die, and from it
> you will be brought out (i.e. resurrected)." (7:25)

Experiences on this earth are a similitude of life in the hereafter.
There seems to be symmetry between our conscious experiences
in this world and our state after death. The following verses
describe resurrection as the ultimate version of existence on
earth:

> And it is Allah Who sends the winds, so that they raise up the
> clouds, and We drive them to a dead land, and revive therewith

the earth after its death. As such (will be) the Resurrection! (35:9).

And a sign for them is the dead land. We gave it life, and We brought forth from it grains, so that they eat of it. (36:33)

He brings out the living from the dead, and brings out the dead from the living. And He revives the earth after its death. And thus will you be brought out [resurrected]. (30:19)

Look then at the effects (results) of Allah's Mercy, how He revives the earth after its death. Most surely He (Allah) will raise the dead to life (on the Day of Resurrection), and He is Able to do all things. (30:50)

O people! if you are in doubt about the raising, then surely We created you from dust, then from a small seed, then from a clot, then from a lump of flesh, some formed and some unformed, that We may make clear (our Power) to you; and We cause whom We please to stay in the wombs till an appointed time, then We bring you forth as babies, then (bring you to growth) that you may attain your maturity (strength); and among you there is he who is caused to die young, and among you there is he who is brought back to the worst part of life, so that after having knowledge he does not know anything; and you see the earth barren, but when We send down on it the water, it stirs and swells and brings forth every kind of beautiful growth. This is because Allah is the Truth and because He gives life to the dead and because He has power over all things. (22:5-6)

And among His signs is this, that you see the earth still, but when We send down on it the water, it stirs and swells: most surely He Who gives it life is the Giver of life to the dead; surely He has power over all things. (41:39)

Everything in existence is eternally etched in the supreme book of creation. This truth was repeatedly revealed to numerous prophets and messenger of the past. From thousands of prophets and messengers only a few are mentioned in the Qur'an. Resurrection, will cover all other animated entities and animals with individual souls or awareness of separation. Resurrection is the final stage before return to the original unity or 'singularity'.

And when the wild beasts will be gathered together; (81:5)

And there is no animal that walks upon the earth nor a bird that flies with its two wings but are communities like you; We have not neglected anything in the Book, then to their Lord shall they be gathered... (6:38)

And (remember) the Day We shall cause the mountains to pass away (like clouds of dust), and you will see the earth as a levelled plain, and we shall gather them all together so as to leave not one of them behind. (18:47)

Paradise used to have a significant place in human imagination and culture until it was lost along with other myths and replaced with hard facts and logic, reducing our horizon of imagination. From ancient times, logos and mythos were together - physics needs the company of metaphysics.

RETURN TO ORIGIN

Truth is one. God is one. In truth, there has always been the ONE and everything is an overflow and reflection of the ONE. In the final phase of the journey, through the hereafter, everything yields to its original elemental roots and unity. The final event is signalled by the first blowing of the trumpet (shock of total destruction and cosmic death). The second blow of the trumpet heralds a return to a new unified life, utter gatheredness and oneness. This is the zone of cosmic unity with no multiplicity. Only God is and was eternal – nothing besides that unique Oneness.

10.1 Identity Meltdown

All diverse creations and realities are illusions and shadows indicating the eternal one Reality. Salvation implies readiness and ease of submission and return to original light, without the personal 'colour' or identity. Earthly experiences, attractions and repulsions were only gross manifestations and metaphors for what is to come after death and subsequent stages of the return.

Oneness and connectedness are discernible states that emanate from absolute unity or singularity. Every creation will lose its short-lived idea of independence and separation from source. Human beings are driven by their soul or essence to awaken spiritually and be in passionate adoration and responsiveness to the Cosmic Soul – God.

> Say: He is Allah, the One and Only—Allah is (Self-Sufficient) on Whom all depend. (112:1-2)

In the Qur'an and Prophetic teachings, two major steps or events mark the end of time and resurrection. One is the end or death of everything in the universe—the first blow—followed by the second blow of resurrection.

10.2 Universal Death, Resurrection and Return to Oneness

The Qur'an refers to the end-of-time events in a manner that there is no clear interval or separation, as time experience on earth. The double blows are referred to as ends and new beginnings. After the first blow and end of all that is called universe comes the second shock, which will make all creatures and people alive and lead them to a gatheredness or assembly. The condition of universal dispersion is now reversed to that of gatheredness.

The two blasts (death and resurrection) are thus described:

And the Trumpet will be blown and behold! From the graves they will come out quickly to their Lord—They will say: "Woe to us! Who has raised us up from our place of sleep." (It will be said to them): "This is what the Most Beneficent had promised, and the Messengers spoke truth!" (36:51-52)

And the Trumpet will be blown, and all who are in the heavens and all who are on the earth will swoon away [as though hit by a thunderbolt], except those whom Allah wills (to be exempt). Then it will be blown a second time and behold, they will be standing, looking on [waiting] (39:68)

Resurrection is the return of life to creation to witness God as the original universal Unity. This is where eternity and the all-pervading Truth are unveiled. Every entity is alive again by grace of the original or supreme light that had been the cause and essence of existence. All notion of separation, differentiation or individuality has now ended. It is as if countless individual drops of water have returned to the ocean of their origin. The loss of the boundary has now resulted in the all-pervading boundlessness and the numerous 'ones' have now returned to the ever present unique One.

Resurrection implies the stage in which the final purpose and journey of creation is fulfilled. This rise signifies union with the primal sacred light, where everything is perfect and beyond description. This phase is the prelude to the ultimate stage of absolute singularity, or 'God only', which is next and last, beyond any notion of creation or time. To establish access to absolute truth, one must deal with relative truth and falsehood in this world. Absolute Truth permeates all. We need to simply surrender to it.

The Prophet Muhammad said, 'Whoever has four qualities will remain in peace on the day of great fear: one who says, "praise be to Allah" for the things he receives; one who says "I ask Allah's forgiveness" upon committing a sin; one who says at the time of trouble, "We are from Allah and to Him we return" and one who asks from his Lord protection and refuge whenever he is afraid of something or is in need'. The Qur'an states:

And do not think Allah to be heedless of what the unjust do; He only gives them respites up to a Day when the eyes will stare in horror—Hastening forward, their heads upraised, their eyes not reverting to them and their hearts vacant—And warn people of the day when the chastisement will come to them, then those who were unjust will say: O our Lord! Give us respite for a little while, (so) we will obey Your call and follow the messengers. (It will be said): did you not swear before (that) there will be no passing away for you!— And you reside in the houses of those who were unjust to themselves, and it is clear to you how We dealt with them and We have made (them) examples to you— And they have indeed planned their (treacherous) Plan, but their plan is known to Allah, though their plan was such that the mountains should pass away (crumble and disappear) — Therefore do not think Allah failing to keep His promise to His messengers; surely Allah is Mighty, the Lord of Retribution— On the day when the earth will be changed into a different earth, and the heavens (as well), and they will come forth before Allah, the One, the Supreme—And you will see the guilty on that day linked together in chains—Their clothes made of pitch and the fire covering their faces. (14:42-50)

10.3 Personal Accountability

Yawm al-Hasarat: the day of despondency and disappointment; on this day, the unbelievers, sinful and disobedient people will feel disappointed regarding their salvation. Everyone will see the results of good and bad works and beliefs in front of him.

(Remember) the Day when every person will come up pleading for himself, and every one will be paid in full for what he did (good or evil) and they will not be dealt with unjustly. (16:111)

The Day where neither wealth nor sons will be of use—Except him who comes to Allah with an intact heart [free from evil]. (26:88-89).

O people! Be afraid of your Lord (by keeping your duty to Him), and fear a Day when no father can do anything for his son, nor a son do anything for his father. Surely, the Promise of Allah is true, so do not let this (worldly) present life deceive you, nor let the chief deceiver (Satan) deceive you about Allah. (31:33).

The Qur'an describes the Day of Judgment as that situation where no one will be able to discuss, negotiate or get help from anyone. People have to face the punishment for their bad deeds and no one will be able to protect them from the wrath of God on that day.

[It will be] the Day when no person will have power (to do) anything for another (person), and the decision, that Day, will be (wholly) with Allah. (82:19).

Woe that Day to the deniers (of Resurrection)! That will be a Day when they will not (be able to) speak-And they will not be permitted to offer excuses! (77:34-36)

The day when the excuses of the wrongdoers will not be of any use, for them there is only the curse and Home of Misery. (40:52)

The believers and pious will be blessed by a light which will engulf them (a soul with no ego tarnish) and the hypocrites will wish they had the guidance of their soul's light. They will be told that it is not possible to go back in time.

On the Day you will see the believing men and the believing women, their light shining forth before them and by their right side. Good news for you this Day! Gardens under which rivers flow, to live there forever! This is the great achievement!— On the Day when the hypocritical men and women will say to the believers: "Look on us! Let us get something from your light!" It will be said: "Go back, and seek the light!" So a wall will be put up between them, with a gate there. Inside it will be mercy, and outside it will be torment." (57:12-13)

We will, without doubt, help Our messengers, and those who believe, in this world's life and on the day when the witnesses will stand forth. (40:51)

The Prophet taught that: 'The hardest moments for the children of Adam are three: the moment they see the angel of death, the moment they will rise up from their graves and the moment they will stand up in front of Allah.'

10.4 Final Gatheredness and Convergence to Unity

'The day of splitting' means the earth will fragment and disintegrate to pieces. People will come out of their graves in haste (instantly) and assemble at a place. The process is known as alhashar and the assembling place is called al-mah'shar. Here the people will stand in front of Allah—Truth—and be judged according to their deeds and beliefs:

> And certainly you have come unto Us alone (as individuals) as We created you the first time. You have left behind you all that which We had bestowed on you. We do not see you with your intercessors whom you claimed to be partners with Allah. Now all relations between you and them have been cut off, and all that you used to claim has vanished from you. (6:94).

> On that day they will follow strictly (the voice of) Allah's caller, there is no crookedness in him, and the voices will be low before the Beneficent Allah so that you will not hear anything except a soft sound [whisper]. (20:108).

> That Day mankind will proceed in scattered groups that they may be shown their deeds—So, he who has done an atom's weight of good shall see it—And he who has done an atom's weight of evil shall see it. (99:6-8)

The Prophet Muhammad said, 'You shall be assembled on the faith you have died on'. He also said, 'You will meet Allah barefoot, naked and uncircumcised'. The Prophet was even asked whether people would look at other's private parts, as they would all be naked. He replied, 'Everyone will be so busy with his own affairs and will not be able to look elsewhere'. *Fitrah*, which means primal code or bringing forth from nothingness implies the imprint of unity. Thus, every human being is born with the innate knowledge of the one source of all creation. The tradition echoes the nakedness of the physical birth by proclaiming that the return back to origin is in a way similar with no cover-ups, physically or otherwise. It is in our 'fitrah' to seek our origin – physically, as in genealogy, as well as in essence, light and unity.

The Prophet also mentioned that at the end of the Day of Judgment, Allah will spread His mercy so generous that even *Iblis* (epithet of Satan) will be expecting mercy from Him.

The end of the world and universe is one of the prime beliefs in Islam. This ending is so important that it had been described by dozens of different names and characteristics described in the Qur'an. Several of these names are often repeated: the end of time, bringing the dead back to life, resurrection, assembling, dissemination, the return, seeing the glory of God, going back to Him. All of creations have emerged from the one unique divine light and will return to the same eternal and sacred source.

Modern cosmologists have produced different theories regarding what will ultimately happen to the universe. In the Closed Model, the universe is expanding but the gravitational force will slow this down and eventually stops the expansion of the universe, after which it starts to contract until matter in the universe collapses to a point, a final singularity termed the "Big Crunch" analogous to the "Big Bang". In the Open Model, the expansion will continue forever to such a point that matter will be so dispersed for any reactions to take place and everything will die slowly. In the Oscillating Universe Model, we are sandwiched in a rhythmical expansion and contraction of the entire universe. This is possible by a big bang-like expansion followed by matter collapsing upon itself due to gravitational forces. This matter then compresses again, due to intense pressures, which can once again cause a big bang. Whilst there are diverse theories to choose from, they all have ends. As human beings we can understand that all events have beginnings and ends; we experience that cycle constantly. The beginning and end of the universe is not difficult to imagine and understand.

10.5 Summary

Absolute truth only appears at relative levels as life on earth, our intellect, knowledge and insights. Truth is like pure light which only appears as dimmed or coloured in the world of experiences. Without real truth, there will be no partial truth or any creation or life experiences. Humanity emerges from the pure light of Divinity and returns to it either by enlightenment or natural death.

> Allah originates the creation, then He will repeat it, then to Him you will be returned. (30:11)

I have had a most fortunate life in being brought up in a culture where birth, life and death were interlinked in a natural way on a daily basis. Several people very dear to me left this earth but kept appearing to me in dreams and visions. One close friend came to my dream a year after his death to ask me to visit his wife the next morning; had I not paid a surprise visit to the lady she would have committed suicide that noon. All was prepared for that ghastly act. Every time I remember my mother, there is a delightful message for me. When my brother passed away, his burial was delayed for three days. I could almost hear him on several occasions with special comments and jokes showing the illusory nature of life on earth and how much better off he is already. For many years now, I have felt the close proximity and closeness of several departed souls. This feeling reduces my own fear or concern for death.

Islam considers death as the event that links what is within time and space to that which is beyond all earthly limitations. It reminds us that the purpose of creation is to come to know the ever-present and eternal Creator. Human beings are created to know, adore and submit to the glory and majesty of this ever-present God, the Lord of the heavens and earth. To love Him passionately is the way for inner reconciliation between self and soul and inspired joyful life irrespective of other circumstances. To love God is to witness His perfections at all times. The ultimate purpose of human life is to attain this state of realisation.

Followers of the Book! indeed Our Messenger has come to you making clear to you much of what you used to hide of the Book and passing over much (leaving out); indeed, there has come to you light and a clear Book from Allah; (5:15)

Without death, birth cannot occur. Without leaving behind the world of matter and mental reasoning, the new world of lights and everlasting joy cannot be realised. Without ongoingness of the soul, hope, freedom and happiness are only short-lived and elusive. Angels are agents that connect the world of energy, matter and human reality with the subtler world of the hereafter and its clear essence and primary patterns. Denials, self-justification and ego delusions are great obstacles to witnessing Reality with its numerous layers and levels. Asking forgiveness and repentance are remedies for denial and egotistic tendencies. The ego/self is deluded and distracted in this life but is also propelled by the power of the soul to break out of the transient and its confusions. Salvation is success in this endeavour, which needs reliance on God and his grace and abandonment of self-concern and egotistic identity.

In Islam, as in most other religions, acts and practices of abstention and withdrawal from usual everyday life are prescribed. Fasting, pilgrimage, giving to the poor, struggle in the way of truth and breaking habits of the self are all part of the Islamic path. The self needs restrictions, outer boundaries, laws and regulations. Only then can the boundless and unrestricted horizons appear – the domain of the soul.

When Allah knows goodness in your heart, He will give you better than that which was taken away... (8:70)

God's presence, justice and judgment are there at all times in this life and the hereafter. The difference is that we can give excuses and be distracted and thereby lose the original purpose for which we were created. After death, we shall face everything as it really is, including our earthly deeds. Thus, if one goes through life with selflessness and spiritual drive, while caring constantly for truth in thought and action, then the hereafter will be experienced with ease. Absolute truth only appears at relative levels as life on earth, knowledge and insights. Truth is like pure light, which only appears as dimmed or coloured in the world of experiences. Without real truth, there will be no partial truth or any creation

> A Messenger, who recites to you the Verses of Allah (the Qur'an) containing clear explanations, that He may bring out those who believe and do good actions from the darkness (of ignorance) to the light (of knowledge). And whosoever believes in Allah and performs good actions, He will admit him into Gardens under which rivers flow, to live there forever. Allah has indeed granted for him an excellent provision. (65:11)

Before time and space or other creations, there was only God and supreme consciousness and light. From that sublime state emanated the universe and all of existence and creation as an overflow and grace. The sparks and beams of energy, which connect multitudes of creations (terrestrial, celestial and sub-atomic), have all overflowed from that original light and are totally dependent upon it until the final return. In truth, there is only that sacred Divine Light and out of its grace, there arose the idea of multitudes of entities and the comings and goings of life and death. The foundation of Islam is the declaration and knowledge that, "There is no god but One". Both time and space have been described in the Qur'an as relative and changeable:

> ..... A speaker among them said: how long have you stayed? They said: we have stayed for a day or a part of a day.... (18:19)

And they remained in their cave three hundred years and increased by [another] nine. (18:25)

Glory be to Him Who made His servant to go on a night journey from the Sacred Mosque to the Remote Mosque of which We have blessed the precincts, so that We may show to him some of Our signs; surely He is the Hearing, the Seeing. (17:1)

And they ask you to hasten on the punishment, and Allah will by no means fail in His promise, and surely a day with your Lord is as a thousand years of what you number. (22:47)

He regulates the affair from the heaven to the earth; then shall it ascend to Him in a day the measure of which is a thousand years of what you count. (32:5)

It was revealed to the Prophet Mohammed that Allah was a hidden treasure and He loved to be known and thus, He created the universe. To know God is to love His attributes and names. The Qur'an reminds us to call upon Allah by these names as needed and as relevant for our needs.

All changes, movements and growth arise from constancy and stillness. There cannot be a lie unless it relates to truth. Absolute truth is where all falsehood, deviations or lies are nonexistent. When all relative realities have ended, so will the idea of separation from the absolute truth and the original singularity; this is the original Godhead or absolute unity. This is the sacred light, which illuminates the entire cosmos as it had been from before the creation of time and space and the illusions of separation and individuality.

The absolute truth cannot be comprehended by a relative mind or experience; it is therefore illogical to discuss it, except through the mist of faith, intuition and inner realisation. This is why the Sufis use the poetic language and mystical symbols. However, even through our intellect we can appreciate the concept that for all the relative existences, there must be an absolute foundation. For every creation, there must be a Creator and with every birth, there is a death. This is why the Qur'an describes the human soul as a ward of the Lord or a special, sacred entity.

At the beginning, there was only God. In the middle, there was only God, who could only be known or realised through the filter of qualities, attributes and varying degrees of understandings and intuitions. Now, once again, at the end of ends, there is only God with absolute and unique brilliance, without a shadow or veil. All the countless lights—lit by the original Light—have now yielded to that absolute Light without any apparent separation, which could only take place in the theatre of space-time. Now everything is back at rest from where it had emerged. Lives, meanings, differentiations and ideas of otherness will all vanish in the light of absolute Oneness. The Qur'an declares:

And to your Lord on that day will be the final return and rest. (75:12)

Death, on a personal and universal level, has brought about a majestic conclusion to a beautiful and glorious creation reflecting the eternal truth of supreme presence of the one Master – Allah. All actions, attributes and subtle forces and entities such as souls, angels, jinns and others have subsided back to Allah. Indeed the whole purpose of the universe was to be exposed to the Divine glories, to adore and worship these attributes and to surrender willingly with contentment and joy.

Allah is the light of the heavens and the earth; The parable of His light is as (if there were) a niche in which is a lamp, the lamp is in a glass, (and) the glass is as it were a brightly shining star, lit from a blessed olive-tree, neither eastern nor western, whose oil almost gives light (even) though no fire touches it— light upon light— Allah guides to His light whom He pleases, and Allah sets forth parables for men, and Allah is All-knower of all things. 24:35)

The above is a description of the enlightened human being. The niche is the breast. The lamp is the soul and the glass is the inner heart. The oil is Allah's grace, mercy and generosity to create the pinnacle of creation – man – to know and to worship Him. This is the overall design of creation and its purpose.

Thus, whoever follows my guidance there will be no fear upon them nor will they grieve. (2:38)

BOOKS

O is a symbol of the world, of oneness and unity. In different cultures it also means the "eye," symbolizing knowledge and insight. We aim to publish books that are accessible, constructive and that challenge accepted opinion, both that of academia and the "moral majority."

Our books are available in all good English language bookstores worldwide. If you don't see the book on the shelves ask the bookstore to order it for you, quoting the ISBN number and title. Alternatively you can order online (all major online retail sites carry our titles) or contact the distributor in the relevant country, listed on the copyright page.

See our website **www.o-books.net** for a full list of over 500 titles, growing by 100 a year.

And tune in to myspiritradio.com for our book review radio show, hosted by June-Elleni Laine, where you can listen to the authors discussing their books.

MySpiritRadio